The
Fantasy
Game

The Fantasy Game

HOW MALE AND FEMALE SEXUAL FANTASIES AFFECT OUR LIVES

Peter Dally

STEIN AND DAY/*Publishers*/New York

First published in the United States of America in 1975
Copyright © 1975 by Peter Dally
All rights reserved
Printed in the United States of America
Stein and Day/*Publishers*/Scarborough House,
Briarcliff Manor, N.Y. 10510

Library of Congress Cataloging in Publication Data

Dally, Peter.
      The fantasy game.

      1. Sex (Psychology)   2. Fantasy.   I.   Title.
BF692.D3   1975   155.3   74-31112
ISBN 0-8128-1790-7

To an inconstant muse

Contents

Preface

This book is about sexual fantasies; how they develop, the
form they take, and most of all their ubiquitous influence on
human behaviour. Sex is no longer a taboo subject, but
many people still feel ashamed of their sexual fantasies, and
some deny that they have them. Yet virtually everyone has
sexual fantasies; how much he or she is aware of them
depends on many things: age, emotion, success, frustrations
and emotional relationships.

The basis of everyone's fantasies is firmly formed by the
age of five, and it never changes, although later embellishments may give the illusion that it does. In general, fantasies are either masochistic, involving submission to someone
else, or sadistic, in which the person is overpowered and
humiliated. Fantasies range from scenes of mild aggression
to extreme cruelty and brutality. The *Oxford English Dictionary* defines both masochism and sadism as 'perversions',
but ultimately everyone can be related through his fantasies
to one of these two extremes.

The masochist in his fantasies needs to be denigrated and
ill-treated, to be captured, stripped, bound hand and foot,
whipped, degraded and defiled, made to plead for pity, and
in extreme fantasies tortured near to death, crucified, raped,
eaten alive, forced to become the despised slave of his tor-
mentors. Sadists fantasize about domination and cruelty:

they imagine themselves causing pain and suffering. Flagellation features large in sadistic fantasies, often enhanced by pornographic writings: the rod, birch, hand and whips of all sizes are frequent images in the mind of the sadist.

In many instances sadism and masochism exist side by side in differing proportions. Probably only a small proportion of people with very extreme fantasies possess these in relatively pure forms. Most 'wise' and level-headed people have well-balanced fantasies of sadism and masochism, which help them to maintain a sense of proportion of events and a firm grasp of 'reality'. Such people are not particularly common: in most people's fantasies one of the two extremes predominates. How people are affected by their fantasies is the central theme of this book. People with strong sadistic fantasies often feel frightened by the power of their fantasies and in consequence develop tight self-control which makes them outwardly inhibited, reserved, distrustful and emotionally cold. They are therefore generally less imaginative and spontaneous than those with predominantly masochistic fantasies.

It is much easier for the masochist, with his fantasy desire for self-humiliation and suffering, to expose himself if need be to others, in contrast to the sadist who is horrified by the idea of anyone discovering the nature of his fantasies. But the differences in the temperaments of sadists and masochists are more complex and fundamental than this. The masochist in his real life compensates for his fantasy desire for punishment. He longs to be the hero or heroine who will save the world, and will endure any necessary sufferings to this end. He hates to cause pain, even though inadvertently he may be responsible for considerable suffering. A sadist can rarely allow himself to grasp initiatives and allow his fantasies to flow outward freely. He is blocked by knowing or sensing that his fantasies are too dangerous to be given a free reign, by the guilt that inevitably follows the pleasure of their satisfaction.

Many people are able to express their fantasies adequately in their everyday sexual relationships, usually with their spouses. All too often, however, marriages fail to develop, or decline and break up, because partners ignore or suppress their own and each other's fantasies, and boredom sets in.

Because so many sexual fantasies cannot be adequately satisfied openly, they may seek indirect expression through work and other apparently non-sexual activities. Idealization frequently disguises masochistic and sadistic fantasies. A man may kill thousands in the name of his country or other ideal. If his fantasies are masochistic his satisfaction comes from feeling that he has helped his country. Unlike the sadist, he derives no pleasure from the suffering he causes. Indeed, he may feel so sorry for the defeated that he subsequently helps them. The soldier with sadistic fantasies, on the other hand, is not motivated so much by the desire to become a hero and save his country as to punish the enemy and inflict the maximum penalties and suffering. Cruelty for its own sake always stems from sadistic fantasies.

It is all too easy to gratify fantasies by such indirect means during wars and social unrest. We have seen this starkly in our own times; the hero leading his people to the promised land as though they were flocks of sheep, the creation of scapegoats – Jews, coloured people, hippies – and the whipping up and manipulation of mass fantasies. From a safe distance we condemn such behaviour. But no man or woman is ever completely safe from the power of his fantasies.

The witch-hunts of the sixteenth and seventeenth centuries, described in the middle section of this book, led to the torture and killing of thousands of people, largely women – a terrible example of the way sexual fantasies may be expressed under the guise of 'doing good'. As the witch-hunting craze died out, men became increasingly preoccupied with the supposed dangers, moral and physical, of masturbation. Social preoccupation with this activity reached a peak in the last half of the nineteenth century and then declined.

Only if we become aware of the power of our fantasies, of the way they may be used both for good and destructive ends, can we hope to avert future outbreaks of mass sadism. Only when we recognize and accept our fantasies, employ them constructively, can we hope to lead fuller lives, and develop more satisfying relationships with one another.

The ideas expressed here are original and based on wide experience and reading. I wish to express my gratitude to all those patients, friends, nurses, students and colleagues who so willingly provided me with material for this book; my long-suffering secretary, Anne Lingham; Richard Seaford of Brasenose College, Oxford, for his expert knowledge of Classical literature; my publishers at Weidenfeld and Nicolson: Robin Denniston whose ideas started the book: Andrew Wheatcroft who brought sense to bear when it was needed: my son, Simon, without whose enthusiasm and suggestions I would never have completed it: Ann Wilson who patiently saw it through to its final form. I take full responsibility for any errors of fact or opinion which may occur.

PETER DALLY
London 1974

1 Fantasies

Where thou and I and liberty have undisputed
sovereignty . . .

E. Brontë

Dr Desmond Morris, author of *The Naked Ape* and *The
Human Zoo*, repaired to Malta with the royalties he received
from his delighted publishers. Undoubtedly he owed a large
measure of his success to the way he placed human sexuality
against a background of the apes. A century ago the French
writer Taine declared, 'Man is a fierce and lustful gorilla.'
The gorilla (although a relatively docile creature according
to zoologists) is frequently the animal most admired by men
and women. Many people like to imagine themselves behaving in an ape-like fashion during sexual intercourse and
see themselves mounting their partners and possessing them
utterly, like Mellors, the gamekeeper in *Lady Chatterley's
Lover*, carrying them away on a flood of grunting, primeval
ecstasy.

Human sexual behaviour certainly involves basic drives
and needs that can be compared with the aggressive and
sexual urges of apes, but there are far more complex factors
at work as well, factors that Desmond Morris did not consider. Admittedly we know comparatively little about ape
thought, but it seems most unlikely that apes are capable of
anything comparable to what is possibly the most important

aspect of our lives – fantasy thinking. The sentiments of self-sacrificing love, pity, bravery, unselfishness and so on may separate us from the apes, but it is the ability to fantasize that puts us at the top of the evolutionary ladder. Without fantasy our lives would be dull, perhaps intolerable and hopeless.

The most obvious example of the fantasy factor is daydreaming. All of us daydream, and when we do we are largely cut off from the outside world and reality. We have all been in the position of being humiliated by an irate superior, or have been conscious of coming off badly in an argument; we lose our tempers and make fools of ourselves. Later we reflect on how much better we might have handled the situation. In our fantasies we relive the episode and see ourselves standing up to the tyrant instead of cringing. Or we imagine everything we could have said, but didn't, and see ourselves demolishing our opponent with devastating retorts. Equally, the office tyrant sits at home of an evening, his children playing happily on his knee, and thinks rosily of the devotion of his well-trained staff.

This kind of fantasy thinking is essential, for it enables us to resolve the inner conflicts created by any sense of humiliation and failure. Without fantasies we would become miserable, neurotic and tension-ridden.

Fantasy thinking often happens without conscious control or direction. Indeed daydreaming can be purposefully directed only to a limited extent. It flourishes best uncontrolled. At a dull meeting the dreamer finds himself drifting away to exotic lands, scaling snow-topped mountains, swimming through coral reefs, acknowledging the applause of admiring millions. Memories and wishes intermingle. Fantasies are readily aroused by frustration and unsatisfied needs. An angry person who has had to hide his or her feelings fantasizes scenes of revenge. A hungry person dreams of food, a thirsty one of sparkling waters, a sexually frustrated one of sex. In such instances fantasy acts as a temporary and partial substitute for the need. Sometimes, when deprivation is extreme, fantasies develop into hallucinations and become 'real'. When the need is satisfied, whether it be by food, drink or sexual orgasm, fantasy disappears.

Freud regarded dreams and fantasies as 'wish fulfilments', coming from subconscious sources. Fantasy thoughts certainly provide an outlet for bottled-up aggression and frustration. They are an important safety valve, allowing us to imagine that we are doing or saying things that in reality are forbidden and/or impossible, and they are especially important in the study of sex and sexual relations. It is this aspect that gives the fantasy factor its fascination.

Virtually no men and very few women can honestly deny that they have sexual fantasies, although many prefer to pretend that they do not. Sexual fantasies take shape in early childhood, become fixed in adolescence or early adulthood, and remain with us until the end of our lives. They evolve in the child's inner world, through his experiences, particularly the way his needs are met and the way he reacts to his frustrations, anger and anxieties, and the nature of his relationships with people close to him – parents, grandparents, nannies and siblings – those on whom he depends for satisfaction, who are responsible in his mind for his pleasures and pains.

The child who feels hungry, uncomfortable and unloved experiences unhappiness and anger. In his own inner world where he is master, he tears and bites at, perhaps even imagines killing, the person he longs to possess, to be united with – usually his mother. Guilt, anxiety and despair follow, for a child cannot clearly distinguish fantasy from reality, and what can be more terrifying than to think yourself responsible for killing the person you love, on whom you depend? Fantasy switches from punishing to being punished, from angry rejection to supplication. Of course every child is frustrated at times. Indeed it is through having to wait for satisfaction that children learn to co-exist with others, to give and take and behave in a socially acceptable way.

It is out of such tumultuous, conflicting emotions that sexual fantasies, masochistic or sadistic, develop, and the patterns of adult sexual behaviour are formed. The child who is forced to suppress outward signs of anger and distress in order to gain parental approval is more likely to have sadistic fantasies than one who feels secure enough to display all his emotions freely. But innate constitutional factors must inevitably exert subtle influences within the continual interaction which goes on between the child and his environment, between his inner and outer worlds.

There is evidence that men and women with sadistic fantasies learn to control their emotional reactions and disguise their feelings earlier than do those who have masochistic fantasies. Only when the boundaries between fantasy and reality break down, either due to exceptional social disruptions, revolutions, wars, or to the effect of drugs and illnesses on the individual, may these childhood controls break down, and allow fantasies and their associated emotions to emerge openly – sometimes, as we shall see, with dreadful results.

Fantasy complicates our sex lives. Through fantasies we can be inhibited or helped, made miserable or gloriously transformed. A man can be promiscuous, engaging in ape-like mounting to bolster a sense of failing power and potency, to express anger and fear, or to combat loneliness and despair. Or he may be celibate, fighting sexual demons like St Anthony in the desert, or like Luther on his hard, cold bed, and he may fear the terrifying fantasies that rise into his consciousness with sexual desire, and therefore avoid sex with a woman. For much of the time sexual fantasies lie hidden, submerged, fearful icebergs whose tips show only now and again. Some people are talkative when they make love, thus keeping the monster at bay. Or they make love in silence, their fantasies flickering in the dark.

There are profound differences between the ways men and women fantasize. Many young women, inadvertently or otherwise, enjoy reading or listening to romances. These stories are certainly not pornographic in the accepted sense, and rarely excite men sexually. None the less they can and do excite women. It is significant that most romantic novels are written for and by women (as most pornography is written by men for men).

Men, on the other hand, are by nature peeping Toms, and voyeurism is an essential aspect of male pornography. Men throw themselves into erotic scenes, and immediately fantasize sexual involvement with the erotic subject. A woman can be aroused by a pornographic scene and may identify with the erotic woman in it. But she doesn't usually imagine herself taking a direct part in the scene itself. Rather she fantasizes a parallel situation between herself and the man she desires. New techniques that excite her are incorporated into making love with her sexual partner.

Whereas most men's fantasies are rapidly aroused by a woman who is no more than a sexual object, most women need to build their fantasies round a romantic partner who wants her for herself as well as her body. Men readily weave sexual fantasies around an idealized Miss World (splendid in bed, perhaps, but imagine having to take her out to dinner). Few women are interested in a Mr World competition; the pectorals of Charles Atlas leave most women cold. But given the appropriate stimulation, a woman's sexual fantasies are as powerful as a man's.

There are infinite varieties of sexual fantasies, but ultimately all are either sadistic or masochistic in content. Sadism is named after the Marquis de Sade, who in his writings glorified the need to inflict pain, if necessary even

6

to murder in the cause of lust. Vice was ennobled and rewarded, virtue humiliated. De Sade divided all human beings into two categories: the predators and the victims. Which a person became depended on temperament and opportunities. De Sade's writings imply that he was a monster of depravity, yet there is no evidence that in his sexual activities he ever went further than flagellation with a few prostitutes. Like many other people who have sadistic fantasies, de Sade was far from being cruel and sadistic in practice. He opposed the death penalty in France and was obsessionally reserved. It was only when he was in prison that his fantasies came to dominate him, probably largely in response to boredom and lack of stimulation. Though some people claim great literary merit for his book, *Justine, ou les Malheurs de la Vertu*, the large majority of people who do not have sadistic fantasies find it a crashing bore.

The word masochism was coined by Richard Krafft-Ebing towards the end of the nineteenth century with reference to the name of the Austrian novelist von Sacher-Masoch. This quite gifted man wrote many stories, most of which described the pleasures of being beaten or humiliated. His most famous tale, *Venus in Furs*, describes how a beautiful woman traps the hero, ties him up, and beats him. 'Maltreat me . . . give me kicks and kisses . . . whip me', implores the hero, wriggling in ecstasy. Today Sacher-Masoch's writings are a good starting-point because the great majority of sexual fantasies are fundamentally masochistic.

Masochistic Fantasies

Masochism is a complex phenomenon. Many lovers enjoy inflicting slight pain on one another during lovemaking and intercourse: biting, hair-pulling, pinching and scratching can be sexually exciting. The psychoanalyst Helene

Deutsch believes that masochism comes naturally to women because they are brought up in the expectation of being penetrated and impregnated. One might think that the corollary of this would be that sadism comes naturally to men, but in fact masochistic fantasies are probably almost as common among men as among women.

The fact that women's fantasies are much more likely to be masochistic than sadistic reflects to some extent the social role of women in our society, although it would be rash to attribute one directly to the other. Certainly the exclusively female function of childbearing can easily become associated with masochism. Masochistic women sometimes fantasize having intercourse while suckling, the two sensations merging. Others identify with well-known big-bosomed women, embracing passivity and fecundity; or with goddesses with full, rounded breasts, such as the Cretan snake goddess. Sexual penetration, impregnation and breast-feeding are strongly linked with masochistic fantasies.

All masochistic fantasies involve submission to someone else, some powerful being. Masochistic women sometimes fantasize being overpowered by a god or satyr, overcome and impregnated, taken into slavery; Greek and Norse myths are often incorporated into their fantasies. Sometimes a hero, an Arthurian knight, Roland, a powerful bull, stallion or ram, or a magical beast like the unicorn does the over-powering. Huge waves and raging seas may fill the fantasy, and Poseidon, the sea god, is usually somewhere in the background. This type of fantasy rarely incorporates the woman's real lover because even in fantasy the combination of the two may seem intolerable or impossible. For such a woman's sex life to be satisfactory, her partner must always seem strong and unassailable in her eyes. An impotent, anxious man stands little chance of becoming her lover.

There is often a close link between ancient myths and sexual fantasies. Are they similar expressions of deep human impulses? Or do they both represent attempts to control and perhaps utilize powerful cosmic forces about which we are still ignorant? An interesting case is that of Antonia.

Antonia was a successful businesswoman, attractive but distrustful of marriage. Brought up in the Middle East, she remembered her Egyptian nanny masturbating her to sleep up to the age of six. When she was twenty-one she became engaged to a Guards' officer. She began to masturbate compulsively, and to dream, fantasizing herself as Osiris, the Egyptian god of the dead, who was murdered by his brother, his body cut up and scattered across the earth. She then became Isis, the sister-wife of Osiris, searching for the pieces in order to reunite them and resurrect her husband. Frustrated and unsuccessful in her search, she masturbated unsatisfyingly. Some three months later, the desire to masturbate suddenly went. Without any convincing explanation she broke off the engagement. This fantasy returned four times more, whenever Antonia was tempted to marry. When she was thirty-five the fantasy sequence was completed: she found all the pieces, and Osiris was resurrected and joined eternally with Isis. Antonia then married a man ten years older than her, 'as dark and tall as Osiris', and the marriage is happy. Fantasies of this kind are singularly free from guilt; pagan gods seem to protect their own.

Less mythological, but similar, are those women's fantasies that are woven round rape, abduction, seduction, white-slave traffic, prostitution. Rape fantasies are particularly common. Claudia fantasizes about being overpowered in various ways, her body exposed to sexual stimulation and attack, to penetration and impregnation. Her sexual excitement reaches a climax as she imagines her pelvis distended by a huge penis and semen pouring into her. Other women's rape fantasies may involve one or several men and women. Negroes, Arab sheiks, powerful princes, burglars, policemen, and, less often, bulls, horses, large dogs and gorillas, are popular fantasy rapists.

It is sometimes said that rape fantasies are popular among women because in a rape situation the woman is blameless. Certainly, helplessness is an important aspect of the fantasy but this is very different from blamelessness. The woman may welcome the fantasy, or it may force itself into her consciousness. Humiliation, pain, distress and orgasm follow, sometimes resulting in real anguish.

Sometimes a previously idealized man becomes associated with sexual fantasies. Women, in contrast to men, never completely desexualize their idealized subjects, and sooner or later may begin to feel sexually attracted to them. Male doctors are particularly at risk in this respect, since they are idealized by many of their female – and not a few male – patients. (The efficacy of any doctor's treatment is always to some extent related to his 'idealism index'.) The nature of the doctor/patient relationship reactivates parent/child feelings on the part of the patient, and sometimes of the doctor. Intimate physical examination and discussion encourage sexual fantasies. The anxieties these may arouse in a woman patient – a fear of being rejected by the doctor, or actually being rejected after revealing her feelings – make it simple for the doctor to be transformed in her fantasies from an ideal into a wicked rapist, from god into devil. Emotional frustration may mount until the boundaries between reality and fantasy break down and the patient accuses the doctor of having raped her. Once she has openly expressed the charge, it becomes increasingly difficult for her to withdraw it. Friends, neighbours and newspaper writers are only too happy to enjoy the drama and perhaps incorporate new ideas into their own fantasies.

Plenty of tragedies have come about through rape fantasies being mistaken for reality: Negroes in the southern states of America have been lynched, men employed by the fathers of sexually frustrated girls dismissed from their jobs. The nuns of Loudon and the female instigators of the Salem witch-hunt are other obvious examples.

The dominant figure in a female fantasy is sometimes an older woman, perhaps with over-large buttocks and breasts (although this is more typical of male fantasies), who encourages and helps in the rape. With fantasies of this nature there is usually an obvious association between such a fantasy female and the way the woman regards her own mother. The content of the fantasy reflects a woman's conflicts over her identity and role, her conflicting wishes to be a child, yet to be sexually free and guiltless.

A common fantasy among middle-class women today, and one that is often acted out in reality, is that of a husband seducing the au pair girl, who in turn is then seduced by his wife. This puts the wife in a powerful bisexual position, which can generate great sexual excitement.

Anal rape may occur as part of a woman's rape fantasy. A powerful man with a large penis may be fantasized, and rape may alternate between vagina and anus.

Oral fantasies usually arise only after reading about or experiencing cunnilingus or fellatio. Cunnilingus is intensely exciting to some women, although after orgasm they may feel dissatisfied if they cannot then experience or fantasize penetration.

A woman whose fantasy is based on impregnation may be unable to fantasize sexually for a considerable time after hysterectomy. Some women have the same experience when they start to take contraceptive pills. In such instances the woman may then become frigid and averse to both intercourse and masturbation. However, such behaviour rarely lasts more than six months, unless there are deeper psychological problems in the woman's background. As fantasies reassert themselves sexual responsiveness returns. None the less, for this to be fully satisfied in intercourse her partner must be able to stimulate her fantasies adequately and at the same time reassure her that she remains sexually attractive.

Jennifer became frigid after her hysterectomy. For twenty-one years she had led what she regarded as a satisfactory sexual life with her husband. After the operation she felt utterly repelled by him and intercourse virtually ceased. A year later she became violently attracted to a neighbour's son, a student of twenty, whom she seduced. She pursued him relentlessly, obsessed with the thought of his ejaculating endlessly into her. When he was away from her she masturbated daily, always with the fantasy of a wild, storm-swept moor, or a raging torrent bursting its banks. Her husband, incapable of understanding her behaviour, left her; later, so did the young man. Eventually Jennifer killed herself by drowning, having unfortunately refused to seek psychiatric help.

Fantasies of being a prostitute usually reveal masochistic and narcissistic needs. A woman may imagine herself to be cold and sexless, giving herself unfeelingly to dozens of men for money, or perhaps forced to do so by a female brothel-keeper. In another type of fantasy, a woman may welcome her lovers, enjoy their embraces, but never be satisfied sexually. Such a woman always has a sense of expectancy in real life, as though she were waiting for the arrival of the ideal man, followed by feelings of disappointment.

A desire for impregnation is usually present in prostitute fantasies. Masochistic humiliation is sometimes extreme, but there may also be sadistic elements. As always, the line between reality and fantasy **may** break down, and fantasy may merge with reality. Excited and over-stimulated by stories of wicked city life, young girls sometimes travel to London and other large cities and literally act out their prostitute fantasies—as pimps know only too well, to their profit.

Some masochistic fantasies incorporate religious elements:

these usually occur only among men who have been edu-
cated by a religious order and women who have had a
convent upbringing. They don't differ in essence from those
outlined above. Bishops and mother superiors feature as
rapists and procurers, aided and abetted by an assortment of
minor clergy, servants and gardeners, all of whom help in
the bondage and humiliation game.

Fantasies of being seduced or forcibly made love to by
other women are normal for lesbians, but are also not uncommon in young women still unsure of their sexual identity, who possess strongly ambivalent feelings towards men
as lovers. Lesbian masochistic fantasies are not basically
different from heterosexual ones. Oral stimulation of the
clitoris and breasts plays a prominent part.

A middle-aged woman has had since puberty a fantasy of
being held down by two older muscular females with large
globular breasts. She is forced to suck each of these in turn
while the women manipulate her clitoris.

Angela, an attractive young journalist, both dreamed of
and fantasized violent lesbian assaults on herself and others
on buses and trains. Eventually tension became so extreme
that she allowed herself to be picked up by a 'butch' and
later raped by her and several of her friends. Angela was
very excited by the experience, yet anxious and guilty. For
some years she felt compelled periodically to repeat the
experience. The fantasy and compulsion disappeared when
her mother died. In later discussions Angela admitted having felt intensely ambivalent towards her mother; she had
always felt an 'angry child' at home and a lonely, rejected/
neglected one when away. She saw the lesbian as an all-
powerful mother figure, draining her of love, at the same
time devouring and absorbing her, causing her to be
remade and reborn.

It is not a particularly common practice for a woman to
insert a dildo or other object into her own vagina or that

of another – either in fantasy or in reality – or at least it wasn't until the arrival of the vibrator on the modern scene.

The idea that women do so derives largely from men's fantasies. Many men are aroused by descriptions and films of women stimulating themselves or each other. They identify with the helpless assaulted woman and become excited by the thought of being attacked by a rapacious female. Some men derive enormous pleasure from being in bed with two women and seeing this fantasy put into practice.

Male masochism follows much the same lines as female masochism, allowing for anatomical differences. A man may imagine himself, unwilling and resisting, overpowered by women, sometimes with the help of men; 'sold as a slave to a cruel queen'; wrecked on an island inhabited only by women; the captain of a ship overpowered by a mutinous female crew. In such fantasies, men are forced by strong relentless females to ejaculate 'against their will'.

The man's masochistic fantasy may centre round manual, vaginal, oral or anal stimulation, or a combination of these. In it the man is both humiliated and yet envied for his 'penis power'. The feature of being forced to impregnate a woman, which is often present, usually disguises sadistic needs.

A variation on this fantasy theme often occurs in romantic and semi-erotic literature, not to mention fairytales. A handsome young man, poor, innocent and virginal, meets in mysterious circumstances a fascinating older woman who is beautiful, rich and clearly aristocratic. She entertains him lavishly for a night, or even a week. He is semi-captive during this time, and is expected to make love frequently to her, not only for her physical satisfaction but in order to make her pregnant. Finally he is dismissed in as strange a fashion as he was summoned, perhaps with a reward. Desperately in love with this ideal woman, he is never able to fall in love again and spends the rest of his life searching

14

for her. Towards the end of his life, he learns that she was
the unhappy Queen of Sheba, who needed a heroic son to
save her country from disaster.

Men and women both respond sexually to this type of
story, told so successfully by an author such as Dennis
Wheatley. Masochistic men readily imagine surrendering
themselves to the queen. Women identify with the queen
and are stimulated by the close all-embracing love of the
young man and his faithful-unto-death attitude.

Rougher, tougher, masochistic fantasies may consist of
being tied up, handcuffed, chained to a bed, hooded or blindfolded, beaten and tortured in various ways and degrees of
severity. Orgasm may be impossible either in masturbation
or coitus, unless the real or fantasy partner swears and uses
obscene words and threats. Both sexes may need to employ
this 'degrading' method of summoning fantasies during
intercourse, to talk of fucking, cunts, pricks, shit, arse and
so on.

Other extreme masochistic fantasies feature men pleading
for mercy, needless to say unavailingly, before one or more
women dressed in leather, gloved and booted, perhaps
masked, armed with whips and sometimes guns. The man
is punished and humiliated by being forced to crawl on the
floor and kiss the woman's boots, and sometimes ends up
being kicked in the teeth, lashed, tied up, handcuffed,
urinated and defecated upon. In some fantasies the latter is
the most important feature, and the man is forced to taste
or eat excreta. Those saints who felt impelled to demonstrate
their love and humility by licking up other people's excreta
and vomit were clearly masochistic apart from other con-
siderations. De Sade, however, was preoccupied by copro-
philia. 'If it is the dirty element that gives pleasure in the
act of lust, then the dirtier it is, the more pleasurable it is
bound to be,' was his rationale.

Pain itself, real or imagined, is exciting to the masochist

only when it occurs in a specially arranged situation, such as exists in fantasy. A masochist no more enjoys pain outside this situation than anyone else. Hence the stereotyped rituals of merciless mistresses clad in black, so frequent in sado-masochistic pornographic writings.

Fantasies of an extreme masochistic or sadistic nature are relatively uncommon, perhaps involving about one per cent of the male population, and considerably fewer women. They always reflect difficulties in relationships, particularly sexual and emotional ones. Many people with such fantasies are able to reach a climax only through masturbation or with an 'object' such as a prostitute. Not a few are impotent. Extreme fantasies may be 'acted out' during masturbation. Typical of such fantasies are scenes of being strapped up and hanged, crucified, strangled to death, shot by a firing squad, severely tortured and perhaps castrated. Castration fears are often expressed in these fantasies.

Richard sees himself lying on a bench with an erection. A woman's hand, without a body, is holding a large cut-throat razor. She begins to shave his thigh and pubic hairs, getting ever closer to his penis. Finally she nicks it and draws blood; he cries out and ejaculates.

Dick's fantasies revolve around cannibalism. He sees himself as helpless, in the power of a hungry woman who is about to devour him. He is very ashamed of such thoughts and tries to blot them out during his infrequent intercourse with his wife. But their compulsive power is such that he frequently takes out prostitutes and pays them to 'eat' him. The only occasions when he can act out his fantasies in the smallest degree with his wife are when he has had plenty of alcohol to drink. He then expects his wife to make love to him, intoning 'snip snap' until he reaches a climax.

Robin, who has fantasies of hanging, imagines the event in vivid detail: his hands and legs are bound, a black hood is put over his head, a rope round his neck, he falls through the floor, his neck snaps, numbness spreads over his body and suddenly culminates in orgasm.

Geoffrey, a businessman, regularly ties himself up, stands naked on a table with a noose round his neck attached to the chandelier and half strangles himself. As the noose tightens his penis becomes erect and he discharges. He uses expensive photographic equipment to record each display. The photographs, which needless to say he always develops himself, provide him with further excitement at bedtime. From time to time an unfortunate man is so carried away by fantasies like this that he kills himself inadvertently, to the distress of his bewildered family. Schoolboys are especially vulnerable to this kind of misadventure because they sometimes form masturbation 'circles' whose experiments become wilder and wilder. A death of this sort occurred a few years ago at a well-known English public school.

Sadistic Fantasies

Sadistic fantasies, which are much less widespread than masochistic ones, are more common among men than among women. They can be every bit as violent as the wildest masochistic fantasies but they also tend to be very much less variable and, consequently, less imaginative. In a typical sadistic fantasy the man imagines himself in a position of power (e.g. a headmaster or a school prefect) and lashes the naked bottoms of the four hundred girls (or boys) under his control, in turn, for some offence they have committed. Dr John Keate, headmaster of Eton, 1809–34, was renowned for the severe floggings he gave his pupils for venial offences. Keate was clearly a sadist. Contrast him with Dr Thomas Arnold at Rugby, 1828–42, who rarely used the cane, and then mainly against boys who had been deliberately untruthful. In fact when he beat a boy in error his 'remorse was pitiful and complete', and he made a public apology to the school. Arnold has the hallmarks of the masochist.

The joys of flagellation have probably always existed. But flagellation reached such a peak of popularity in Victorian times, and so many London brothels catered for the demand, that it became known as *le vice anglais*. It is difficult to find out whether the English really do enjoy the titillations of flagellation more than people of other nationalities. Among the English themselves, flagellation is especially likely to be enjoyed, actively or passively, by those who have gone to boarding school at an early age. The experience of being caned, and until comparatively recently most English schoolboys were, particularly by a schoolmaster whose sadistic fantasies are aroused, must have led to pain becoming associated with sexual pleasure in many cases. Rousseau has told us clearly of the delicious, although painful, sensations he had when beaten by the pastor's sister at the age of twelve. Swinburne had an even greater need to be whipped, a need that may well have had its roots in the birching block of Eton. Edmund Wilson in fact claims that Swinburne's masochism is one of the clues to the Victorian age and its sexual culture, a culture that forced its elite to identify pain with early sexual experiences. Certainly although many women enjoy gentle smacks, few enjoy vicious beatings.

The violence of sadistic fantasies will often cause people to disguise them in various ways. Disguised sadism may be acted out by both sexes. A 'cock-teasing' woman may arouse a man to a pitch of excitement and then leave him standing on the pretext that intercourse is morally wrong. Some of these women end up being assaulted, and even killed, and there is probably a masochistic element in their behaviour. Similarly, a man may make love to a woman and stop before she reaches her climax, saying he feels exhausted or is afraid of making her pregnant. Or he may ostentatiously not ejaculate during intercourse, and later masturbate openly beside her.

Many fantasies centre round such themes. Maggie has a fantasy of letting a man make love to her while she smokes and reads a paper. He is unable to reach a climax and asks her to masturbate him. Continuing to read, she stubs out her cigarette on his erect penis and immediately achieves orgasm herself.

Fantasies of scratching, biting and even eating another person's body are common to both men and women, although extremely sadistic scenes feature mainly in the fantasies of men. Allan, a teenage boy, has a fantasy about his headmaster's wife. He locks her in a small room, tears off her upper clothing and sucks and bites her breasts while she cries and begs for mercy.

Some men, and a few women, have fantasies of killing or injuring another person. Ever since reading *Othello* as a schoolgirl, Helen has been sexually excited by the thought of strangling a powerful but helpless Negro. His struggles heighten her excitement, and she reaches orgasm when she feels his body going limp. Judith has a fantasy of a headless man standing before her with an erect penis. She lies on her bed without moving or touching her genitalia, her thighs pressed tightly together, and reaches a climax at the same time as the headless man's penis ejaculates.

Variants on Fantasizing

Sometimes pornography is used to absorb fantasies and partially hide their presence. Since Aubrey was nine he has masturbated while looking at photographs and drawings in soft porn magazines, imagining himself copulating with the women shown there. He has never considered them to be real people, nor has he ever related them to anyone he knows. When he was twenty-three he tried to make love to his fiancée, but was impotent. A year later, still impotent, he asked for medical help. He denied having sexual fantasies, and emphasized that he always used pornography to masturbate. He was shocked by the idea of comparing his fiancée to the pornographic women. 'They've nothing in common,' he said repeatedly. 'Those women aren't real.'

Writing down a fantasy and subsequently reading it as a pornographic story is a popular means whereby people distance themselves from their fantasies. David types out his fantasy (it takes more than two hours and covers eight foolscap sheets, all of which are torn into tiny pieces after orgasm) and then slowly reads it aloud to himself, masturbating all the while. Not unrelated to this technique is the sending of anonymous poison-pen letters combining obscenity with sadistic threats. A man may write such a letter during a state of high sexual excitement to an 'abandoned, perverted' woman, with whom he is only slightly, if at all, acquainted. Newspaper accounts of divorces or scandals of a sexual nature provide a fund of names and addresses for the writer. Semen and faeces are sometimes smeared across the pages, adding to the writer's sadistic excitement.

Men who make anonymous telephone calls to women picked at random from the telephone book are motivated by similar needs and fantasies, and by fears of impotence and direct involvement with women. This type of man lacks imagination and is able to masturbate enjoyably only by creating and acting out a fantasy situation. Verbal penetration is as much as he can manage, and only then at a safe distance. He is invariably grossly inhibited, obsessional, humourless and timid in his everyday life. His fantasies are often stimulated by accounts in the newspapers of missing or murdered children and may then take the form of obscene telephone calls to the unfortunate parents. Like the poison-pen letter writer, his fantasies are sadistic.

People who indulge in graffiti are rather different. Public lavatory graffiti are more often homosexual than heterosexual, although this is true to a lesser extent in women's lavatories. Male graffiti are frequently enlivened by drawings of huge penises and testicles, or over-large buttocks and breasts, which have a crude if simple humour. One man always gets rid of his frustrated feelings when disenchanted with his workmates by writing on the walls of a lavatory at work. He describes and draws his foreman's genitals, and offers advice about what should be done to put them right and who among his mates should assist in the task. Another young man inscribes on lavatory walls the name and telephone number of any girl who refuses or humiliates him.

Voyeurs are always male, although many women have voyeuristic fantasies. Peeping Toms lack the ability to fantasize easily, perhaps because their sexual fantasies are of a sadistic nature. They find sexual excitement by peeping through uncurtained windows at women undressing, watching them urinate and defecate, and staring at couples making love in public parks or swimming pools. Many arm themselves with expensive binoculars. Not a few of these voyeurs remember feeling excited as children at the sight of their mother or sisters on the lavatory. The fact that the woman or couple being watched is unknown, and unaware of the voyeur, is usually important; the voyeur is then able to project his fantasies on to them and masturbate to completion. However some voyeurs require the extra excitement of being discovered and chased in order to raise sexual tension high enough to have an orgasm. Most voyeurs are harmless.

Fantasizing in front of a mirror is popular with both sexes and sometimes goes on for many hours. A woman may be interested only in watching her breasts, which she fondles, or sucks if they are large enough, pushing them into certain shapes and elaborating a tale round them. A man may gaze admiringly at his erect penis in the mirror, overestimating its length and breadth, visualizing the reactions of observers. It is only one step from here to exhibitionism in public. Sometimes the mirror fantasizor splits himself into several people, male and female, who stimulate each other by mutual masturbation. Penis size features in the fantasies of many men and not a few women. Many sexually unsure men express their fears of impotence in preoccupation with the size of their penises.

Pornography, which among other things allays neurotic sexual fears, is often preoccupied with penises: 'He had a smaller than average penis, eight and a half inches long and about as round as the middle of a milk bottle [note the association]. He was never able to bring Mildred to a climax . . .' – until he fitted rubber piping over his penis. In fact, of course, provided a man's penis is not deformed and is able to erect, an inch or two either way makes virtually no difference to his ability to satisfy his partner.

Disguised forms of sexual fantasies include arson and shoplifting. The arsonist often admits to sadistic fantasies that began long before puberty, and to setting fire compulsively to paper and inflammable materials, especially women's clothes, during his childhood. After puberty fire becomes intimately related to masturbation. Sooner or later the arsonist's fantasy may be acted out in real life. He then finds masturbation fully satisfying only while watching a fire he has begun, or recalling its details a short time later. A combination of guilt and desire to identify with the firemen sometimes compels the arsonist to show himself openly at the fire, pretending to be an innocent bystander anxious to help. It is extremely difficult to alter such fantasies (although behaviour therapy of the kind used in *A Clockwork Orange* may be effective), and in the absence of treatment an arsonist is unlikely to lose his compulsion before old age.

Some women have fantasies of hideous, fat, repulsive

men, smelly and unkempt. And some men have fantasies of squinting, ugly women (the squint creates the illusion that the squinter can see through you), women over-endowed with enormous thighs and bosoms, sweaty women, menstruating women, very old women, female infants, schoolgirls in pigtails, dead or unconscious women.

Captain Y can make love to his wife only when her face is covered by a black cloth. He then imagines that she has died from a mortal wound in her groin. From before puberty he has had exciting fantasies of nude, unconscious women, clothed only in sanitary napkins, whose bodies he has to 'lay out' in bizarre postures. He is obsessively interested in photographs of dead women. Recently he was greatly excited by pictures in a Sunday newspaper of a bull elephant trying to revive a dying female by mounting her.

Jim imagines himself to be a powerful magician 'like Merlin', standing on top of a mountain, looking down on the world. A torrent of urine pours from his penis, flooding the land. He watches people swimming for their lives in the deluge he has created, thousands drowning. They resemble 'absurd ants', and are all in his power. The orgasmal climax occurs after violent thunderstorms and a terrible earthquake. Such a sadistic fantasy may have been in Swift's mind when he wrote *Gulliver's Travels*. The event that provokes Gulliver's hasty departure from Lilliput occurs when he extinguishes a fire in the queen's palace by urinating over it. He is expelled from the country for this (indeed he is nearly prosecuted for it) because one of the strictest laws of Lilliput is that it is absolutely forbidden to urinate within the precincts of the queen's palace.

Homosexual fantasies are quite common. Although confirmed homosexuals, men and women, almost always have homosexual fantasies, people who have homosexual fantasies are not necessarily 'queer'.

Ted, an ambitious young advertising man, masturbates

compulsively after every board meeting. His fantasies are always the same, of being held down and raped by several men, some naked, others dressed as women. Yet Ted is essentially heterosexual in real life. His fantasies express a deep-rooted sense of insecurity and a fear of failure. In his case masturbation always follows mental battles with his male colleagues at work. For Ted there is a clear relationship between power and sex, and he masturbates in order to relieve his anxieties.

Fetishism

Fetishism, by and large a male phenomenon, usually includes elements of both sadism and masochism, although rarely to a marked degree. The fetishist's fantasies always revolve round his fetish object. But often he acts out his fantasy, at first alone and then perhaps with a prostitute or willing partner.

The fetish object substitutes for a sexual partner, and as such is intensely exciting. All fetishists are more or less fearful of intercourse, and the fetish protects against this anxiety. Fetishes, like the more extreme forms of sado-masochism and homosexuality, are incorporated in sexual fantasies early in childhood, probably well before the age of nine. Most fetishists are able to recall being fascinated by and receiving pleasure from their fetish objects before this time. A man of twenty, whose sexual fantasies drive him to cut off girls' hair, has been aware of this compulsion since he was six, when he remembers the pleasure of smelling and cutting his cousin's hair. A middle-aged single man has had a fantasy since his late teens of being dressed in young girl's clothing, pushed in a pram by a large woman, seated on and covered by a rubber sheet. He can recall his interest in rubber sheets and prams from as early as five years old.

Rubber sheets and garments are popular fetish objects. The fetishist often visualizes himself in tight black shiny rubber garments, sometimes in bed with a woman similarly encased (but ingeniously able to have intercourse). The mere thought of being dressed from head to toe in rubber is sexually arousing to such a person. One rubber fetishist can never read about frogmen without compulsively masturbating. Another rubber fetishist with masochistic fantasies always imagines himself being attacked and beaten by rubber-clad figures. Most rubber fetishists are heterosexual, but they have difficulty in making love to their partners, and certainly in enjoying sexual intercourse, unless some rubber is present to stimulate their fantasies. They may insist on making love only on a rubber sheet, or while wearing rubber or plastic pants. Frequently they try to persuade their partners to wear rubber. (Many women, understandably, find it difficult to comprehend and accept fetishism. 'I'd much rather he had an affair with another woman than dress up in all that kinky array. I could understand that,' remarked a long-suffering wife.)

Rubber and plastic mackintoshes, especially black shiny ones, are the main standby for many fetishists. The number of rubber fetishists in Britain and the USA must be considerable to judge from the number of advertisements inserted in newspapers and magazines to catch their attention.

Furs, satins and soft silky materials are also popular fetish objects among men, and perhaps some women. However the sexual excitement felt by a woman dressed only in a fur coat or hat, or silk dress, often stems from how she thinks her partner will react to seeing her so dressed. None the less excitement may be great enough to cause her to masturbate.

An unusual fantasy concerning fur was described by Solomon, a middle-aged accountant. He had been excited by the feel of fur since an occasion in his childhood when his mother, wearing a fur coat, had hugged him. As an adult he could be potent only by imagining himself covered by a fur rug, and to help his fantasy he kept one on his bed. Shortly after he was married a piece of fur was pulled from the rug by accident, and was on the table when he ate breakfast. Solomon found the erotic experience resulting from the juxtaposition of egg and fur intense. His fantasy changed quite suddenly into a scene of himself seated nude at a table on which were scattered pieces of fur. He reached across the table and 'accidentally' knocked a lump of fur on to his lap. His fantasy extended so much into his everyday life that eventually he found it difficult to endure even a business luncheon without the presence of fur.

Shoe fetishists are attracted by the shape, colour and feel of the shoe, and particularly by high heels. These female 'phallic objects' symbolize sexual rapaciousness and sadism to the fetishist. 'You can feel that shoe squeezing you, the heel digging into you,' explained one man.

Martin, a middle-aged man, has a fantasy of a tall slim woman, naked except for black shiny shoes with stiletto heels some six inches high. She walks slowly towards him, smoking. He backs away but she follows, pushes him to the floor and threatens to tread on his body. Finally she makes him take off her shoes and put them on his own feet. They are invariably too tight, but their pressure brings on orgasm.

Clearly some of the popularity of *Cinderella* stems from this fetish (though there are other more important themes in the fairytale). Freud would have called the ugly sisters transvestite shoe fetishists.

Women's slippers were popular fetish objects during the nineteenth century (Flaubert probably had a mild slipper fetish), but they now seem to have lost much of their charm. So have gloves, although black, opera-length gloves still feature in male fantasies. 'She wore glossy black gloves, almost up to her shoulders. In one gloved hand she grasped a cruel-looking birch, in the other she held a thick rubber truncheon. . . .' Women's hats and bras seem never to have got into the top ten, but black mesh stockings and suspender belts are as much in demand as shoes.

Transvestism

Fantasies of dressing in female clothing (transvestism) probably occur in as much as five per cent of the male population; they range from featuring single garments to complete female regalia, wig and make-up. Most transvestites at some time or another put on the clothes for which they have a yearning and masturbate. The feeling of the clothing on their bodies, combined with their fantasies, is sexually exciting.

For most transvestites the clothes need to have been worn by a woman before they can be fully arousing. New clothing tends to be unexciting, and most transvestites start by wearing garments belonging to their mothers or sisters. Sometimes the transvestite feels compelled to steal women's clothing from a washing line or even, in extreme cases, to break into a house. It is almost as though the transvestite has to steal love. He must bolster up a neurotic sense of sexual superiority over women, otherwise he will be impotent. When he puts on female clothing the transvestite becomes both a woman and a potent male in his sexual fantasy.

Transvestite sexual fantasies commonly follow a pattern. Paul visualizes a walk in the country. He passes a house, the door of which is open. Feeling thirsty he goes in to ask for water, but no sooner does he enter than the door shuts with a bang and he is attacked by three women. He is overpowered, undressed, ridiculed. Then, to his horror, one of the women proposes that he should be dressed up in their clothing. He feebly resists, but horror gradually gives way to sexual excitement at the feel of the underwear. He suddenly realizes that he longs to dress as a woman and be accepted as such by other women. He explodes in ecstasy as the truth is revealed to him, and he and his erstwhile attackers become intimate friends.

Jonathan's fantasy is of his wife forcing him to wear her clothing. When he at first refuses she threatens to leave him for another, more potent man. He gives way and allows himself to be dressed up as a woman. His wife then forces him to lie on his back and rapes him, to her (and his) complete and intense satisfaction.

In ordinary life transvestites show no outward signs of their fantasies, although some regularly wear female underwear. The majority are heterosexual, but few wives are able to accept a transvestite husband. They feel helpless, having no sexual rival to compete with. Marital sex is upset, for the wife's new-found concept of her husband inevitably disturbs the flow of her own fantasies. And homosexual fears and fantasies may be brought to the surface. Many a transvestite's wife has sought reassurance and escape from her fears through an extramarital affair.

'Drag' parties provide outlets for those transvestites who feel compelled to show themselves off in public, and for those with homosexual traits. Prostitutes and call girls provide the main means of acting out if masturbation alone is insufficient to relieve the transvestite's needs.

Giles, a married man in his thirties, regularly seeks out a particular prostitute. In her room he dresses as a woman. The couple then go out and call upon another, younger, prostitute. She has been naughty and aunty (Giles) is asked to punish her. He spanks her, and she weeps and begs forgiveness. He grants this, she throws herself gratefully upon him and they have intercourse.

Mirrors may provide an answer for some transvestites, as they do for other people's sexual needs. Jones regularly dresses in frilly female underwear and makes himself up to look, in his eyes, like an attractive young woman. He then stands in front of a large mirror and imagines himself walking in the park, admired by passing men. One man stops, slowly approaches and unzips his trousers to reveal a large erect penis. The man now passes through the mirror and Jones feels himself embraced and penetrated. At that moment he ejaculates. Sometimes he stands in front of the mirror, dressed above the waist as a woman, below the waist as a man. He then photographs the reflection of his penis in the mirror. Looking at himself and, later, the photographs gives him a sense of enormous power and potency.

This example illustrates how men with transvestite and fetishist fantasies can split readily into two or more personalities when sexually excited. But sometimes such people are not able to distinguish fantasy from reality, and the social and legal consequences may be serious for them.

Transvestism is much less frequent in women and is more associated with lesbianism. In fact most women who dress in men's clothes probably get none of the sexual thrill from contact with the clothing itself that male transvestites do. There are famous examples of women masquerading as men: in our own time, Vita Sackville-West sometimes assumed the guise of 'Julian' with Violet Trefusis. Most of them cross-dress to express their masculine role in a homosexual relationship. For the rest male attire symbolizes rejection of the feminine role and, in a few, expresses a wish to change sex.

Transsexualism

Transsexualism is very different from transvestism. The male transvestite has no desire to change his sex; he seeks only to *dress* as a female. He remains a man even when he becomes outwardly a woman. The transsexual on the other hand wants to change sex. He or she experiences no sexual thrill from wearing clothing of the opposite sex. In fact most transsexuals are singularly lacking in sex drive.

Jean is twenty-one. She is tall, plump, intelligent, outwardly placid and quite attractive. From the age of six she has had fantasies of herself on horseback, dressed in armour, leading a mighty army into battle. Soldiers address her as 'My Lord'. She is invincible with a sword. During war she challenges the enemy leader to personal combat and vanquishes him. Jean's fantasy sometimes continues for hours, especially after she goes to bed at night. Only occasionally does it culminate in orgasm; for this to happen she must kill the enemy leader. Jean's Joan of Arc-type fantasy reflects her sadistic conflicts and needs.

Transsexuals of both sexes often demand sex-change operations. Technically this is not particularly difficult, although not many plastic surgeons or theatre nurses are willing, for personal and psychological reasons, to oblige. The results, although occasionally satisfying to people like Jan Morris, are often far from good. Reality may not match up to fantasy and depression may set in. A lifetime's ambition is suddenly removed and the psychological adjustment required following the sex change is often too great for the transsexual's resources.

Sexual Perversion

A perversion is 'an unnatural act'. But what is unnatural depends on what society regards as normal and abnormal. Between two consenting adults, all sexual behaviour is acceptable and is therefore normal for them. A sexual pervert offends other people by his behaviour, and is liable to be punished if society regards him as an undesirable deviant.

Sexual perverts are usually men. Their fantasies, which are in keeping with their particular perversions, were formed long before puberty and do not undergo much change with time. They are curiously unimaginative people and their fantasies frequently reflect this.

Vincent, a pederast, masturbated to a memory from his ninth birthday party when he wrestled with a younger boy. As an adult he often invited boys to his home on various pretexts, but not until he was twenty-nine did he meet a boy who encouraged mutual masturbation. From then on his compulsion grew and he assaulted children who were unwilling to co-operate. Masturbation became a second-rate activity after this first real experience. When the compulsion was strong he saw every child he passed as a potential partner, as someone 'who can trust me'.

The pervert's ability to separate his fantasies from the outside world is never strong and it virtually disappears when sexual tension is high. Masturbation and the perverse act become one. Like a small child who breaks a cup and blames 'the black man who came down the chimney', the pervert may offer a naïve explanation of his action that reflects a poor sense of reality rather than deliberate lying.

We do not *know* why a person should become a pervert, or how his fantasy sexual object becomes 'real' to him. But because it is 'real', it is 'natural' for him and he doesn't feel he is doing wrong. The exhibitionist, for instance, virtually believes he is giving his victim pleasure, that he is doing her a favour by exposing himself.

Perverts are lonely, obsessional, withdrawn people, unable to form satisfying relationships with others. Their fantasies are invariably of a sadistic nature. During adolescence they masturbate, often compulsively, from anxiety and loneliness. Their associated sense of guilt about their sexual behaviour is never strong and gradually fades with time. Constant repetition of the fantasy through masturba-

tion brings it ever closer to reality. Given a highly vulnerable personality, masturbation may play an important role
in the evolution of sexual perversions. Absence of guilt
about the fantasy means that there is little or no motivation
for erecting strong psychological barriers, for strengthening
those aspects of character that might help to keep fantasy
from becoming reality.

It is sometimes claimed that suitable pornography will
help sex perverts to control their impulses.

Joe is an exhibitionist, and several times has been caught,
put on probation and fined. He always chooses young girls
in front of whom to exhibit himself. He has a large collection of hard pornography, books, magazines and photographs, mostly on the subjects of bondage and flagellation.
For most of the year he is content to read these and masturbate. But sooner or later he notices a particular girl in the
street. He becomes preoccupied by her image and eventually
becomes 'impotent', unable to masturbate. It is now that he
goes out and exposes himself. After this 'catharsis' he is able
to revert to his formerly satisfying ways. Pornography, in
his case, does not prevent or cause his exhibitionism.

Sexual fantasies vary from banal scenes of intercourse with
one or more people to the most complicated, bizarre, unvarying sequences of events. Although individual fantasies
differ widely, most are remarkably dull and unimaginative,
except to the person who has them.

Fantasies are usually either 'sadistic', where the person
plays or identifies with an active, aggressive role, or 'masochistic', where the person's role is passive and submissive.
Many people's fantasies contain a mixture of both, although
one element usually predominates. Masochism is more common than sadism, particularly among women. Fantasies can
be predominantly heterosexual, homosexual or a mixture.

Of course there are many kinds of fantasy, apart from

those of a sexual nature, that influence personality and behaviour and contribute to imagination and the drive to succeed. Sexual fantasies themselves may be combined with and expressed through other fantasies, each then being liable to exaggerate and distort the other's form and force. Dangerous as this may sometimes be, it is more likely to produce a spontaneous imaginative personality than when sexual fantasies are suppressed.

2 The Effects of Sexual Fantasies on People's Lives

Were it not for imagination, sir, a man would be as happy
in the arms of a chambermaid as of a duchess . . .
Samuel Johnson

Sexual fantasies are often so extremely sadistic or masochistic, or may seem so comical when described, that people are usually reluctant to admit to or describe them. Today most men and women will freely confess to having masturbated at some time or another, but few are prepared to disclose the nature of their fantasies, whether to a psychiatrist, priest, spouse, lover or best friend. In some ways they are right not to do so. To know someone's sexual fantasies is to comprehend a large part of that person and his needs. Sexual fantasies are intimately related to people's personalities. One can be gauged with a fair degree of accuracy from the other.

One of the most interesting ways in which sexual fantasies affect our lives is in our choice of job. Of course it is necessary to go carefully with a subject such as this and avoid making the glib assumption that everyone's choice of work is influenced by his sexual fantasies. To describe every detective as a sadist, or every fireman as a would-be-arsonist, would be a slick and easy way of summing up the hundreds of complex factors that make up a human being. It would also be wrong. Nevertheless, although chance and choice obviously play a part in men's and women's types of work (and although many people, especially those in semi- or unskilled jobs work largely to earn money and to fill an accepted place in society), fantasies undoubtedly exert an influence that is often strong and not consciously realized.

Sexual fantasies develop out of the experiences of the child in his early years. In turn they influence his later life, his choice of partner, his character and social behaviour and the nature of his work and interest. The most common sexual fantasies are sado-masochistic. In a sense this is reflected in the way our society organizes itself. Power flows from the top to the bottom, through a network of departments. Whether a man works for the army, the police force, a commercial firm or the civil service, he is usually in a position of some power: he issues instructions to people who are expected to carry them out; he himself is given orders. Some people like to have more power than others and are constantly struggling to acquire it. Others are satisfied to remain where they are, secure and content. The more extreme a person's fantasies, the greater their influence is likely to be.

Sadists and Masochists

Although it is difficult to draw an exact dividing line between people with sadistic and those with masochistic fantasies, broadly speaking the difference is that the masochist's inner need for humiliation gives him a greater driving-force in most aspects of his life. The sadist tends to be much more aware of the unacceptability of the violence in his fantasies, and compared to the masochist is more frightened and inhibited by them, a characteristic that spills over into his everyday life.

Men and women with masochistic fantasies are more liable

to suffer bouts of incapacitating depression than those with sadistic fantasies. Their self-confidence needs to be constantly boosted by success in work and/or love to counterbalance their underlying sense of failure, guilt and fantasy desire for punishment. The masochistic businessman of ability feels he must succeed. His compulsion to do so is sometimes so great that everything else is excluded and he virtually becomes a megalomaniac. The ambitious, successful politician, the creator of a great industrial empire, the unscrupulous scientist stealing a march on his colleagues – all experience essentially masochistic fantasies, which are directed towards making them a hero and saviour. It is easier for the masochist to adapt his life in socially acceptable ways than for the sadist. The masochist longs to be a hero, to conquer and save the world, to earn the praise and admiration of his mother (or her father) – whether the parent is dead or alive – in whatever career he pursues, and eventually to replace the parent. This gives him his dynamism, for the man who has strongly masochistic fantasies is likely to be forceful and aggressive, and often ruthless in his work. In his sex life he may be a 'Casanova', needing to be liked and wanted by women. He may embark compulsively on affair after affair; repeated success is required to compensate for his masochistic fantasies, and for his underlying need to submit to and please women. Yet he remains devoted to all women, and most of them to him. At the centre of his emotional life, radiating their influence over and beyond his childhood, are usually a dominant mother and, later, a dominant wife.

People with sadistic fantasies have strong self-control. They often appear to be inhibited and to lack spontaneity, and they do not easily open themselves up to other people or trust them. A masochist usually dislikes inflicting pain or condoning sadistic behaviour since he identifies with the victims, feels for them as human beings, and sympathizes with their sufferings. Yet he retains a sense of perspective. The sadist, whose inhibitions 'protect' him from his fantasies, may also rail against torture and suffering, but in a much wider, sometimes ludicrous way; even to the extent of hesitating to kill a fly. Other sadists defend themselves against their fantasies by whipping up and joining public crusades against any scapegoat to hand, be it homosexuals, pornographers or Asiatics. Or they may call vociferously on the authorities to bring back hanging and flogging. Much of the outcry against fox-hunting (apart from overtones of class), and the horror expressed at this highly ritualized sport, is an expression of people's fear of their own sadistic fantasies. Yet the vast majority of people with sadistic fantasies organize their lives in such a way as to live acceptably in society, and at the same time manage to provide reality outlets for their fantasies. They are often found in jobs that involve little human contact, where human beings are relegated to an in-tray of forms or financial accounts, or where their control over others is limited by strict regulations. People who enjoy this kind of work have little interest in becoming heroes.

Masochistic females *search* for a hero. But all too often the hero turns out to have feet of clay, and disappointment, even despair, ensues. One affair may quickly follow another. Margot, aged thirty, has been married twice, had two other serious affairs, during each of which she lived with the man concerned for over a year, and innumerable minor sexual engagements. She becomes infatuated with a man who, at the time, appears to be perfect. Attached to him (she is extremely attractive and does not find attachment hard to come by), she feels emotionally secure and happy. Within a month or two the idealization starts to crumble. She sees that her hero really has feet of clay. Desperately she tries to blot out reality, and to force the man into a heroic mould. Not unnaturally, he resists and the affair or marriage breaks apart at the seams. Multiple orgasms give way to frigidity, anxiety and despair.

Sometimes a woman will try to avoid being hurt again by deliberately looking for unheroic qualities in the men who show interest in her. When she does find a hero, someone who has those qualities that satisfy her fantasy needs, she may become sexually demanding, craving continually to be overpowered and impregnated. Others may join Women's Lib, or toy with lesbianism, trying their best to denigrate the hero. 'Men are such insecure creatures that if they are not using their big stiff pricks they don't feel they are really male. Most of them feel that women are only invented to make them feel more male . . .' is a cry from the female masochist's heart.

Desire for children stemming from masochistic fantasy is sometimes overwhelming. Many a large family is founded upon masochism. Joan has had eight children. She refuses to take a contraceptive pill on the unsupported grounds that it 'will destroy my femininity, do untold harm to my insides'. Indeed, once when she contemplated taking the pill, she 'felt sick before even swallowing it'. In each of her last three pregnancies she considered abortion, encouraged by her husband, but each time she virtually blackmailed him into 'persuading' her to have the child. 'He is so forceful. What can I do but have his children?' she explained.

Occasionally a woman will select an unattainable, usually unwilling, hero, fall madly in love with him and imagine that he is in love with her. This foible – 'erotomania', or the Divine Passion – mostly affects married women.

Rachel became convinced that a certain bishop was in love with her. She wrote him long passionate letters, and on a number of occasions went to call on him at his palace. She realized that 'he must be discreet because of his position', but she 'knew' that he communicated with her indirectly through his sermons and public utterances. She collected these and underlined his messages. At night, and particularly in the early morning, she felt his body pressing down upon her. At such times, 'when he is thinking of me', she had to struggle to ward off erotic thoughts, which she regarded as unworthy of her love. Rachel had married a handsome, intelligent solicitor who was successful in his work, an up-and-coming local politician, a sought-after public speaker, but lacking in sex drive so far as his wife was concerned. Increasingly frustrated, she became mentally ill and deluded.

Masochists of both sexes counter depression in a variety of ways: by working ever harder for success, in promiscuity, gambling, drinking. Most alcoholics and chain smokers, for instance, have masochistic fantasies. Inside every male alcoholic is a hero, hammering ineffectually to get out. Many an alcoholic in his cups is about to do great things. He is misunderstood, his intentions are blocked, people are obstructive, mean and malicious. Occasionally, an alcoholic succeeds in the arts, politics, one of the professions, business. But sooner or later his heroic success dissolves and he sinks into egotism and misery. The alcoholic's wife often sticks by him through thick and thin, enduring misery and privation for the sake of her hero. She mothers him and he responds with angry childish outbursts. Female alcoholics are commonly married to or closely involved emotionally with successful men. Having searched for and found her hero, the woman may then find herself ignored by him, or idealized and relegated to a pedestal. Alcohol lessens resentment, sometimes embarrasses the hero, and points to the woman's sense of despair and helplessness.

Naturally, masochistic men and women do sometimes become heroes. Albert Schweitzer probably had masochistic fantasies and strove to be a saviour to his natives. Jesus can be said to have acted out masochistic fantasies on the cross and thus became a saviour.

Christianity is of course essentially a masochistic religion – we are all miserable sinners deserving punishment. But it is almost impossible to imagine a lasting religion founded by a sadist (although sadistic rituals and ceremonies inevitably become incorporated in any religion). The Jewish god of the Old Testament is at times terrifying and apparently cruel and ruthless. But all his actions are directed to the good of his chosen people; none is sadistic for its own sake. It seems natural enough that religions should be based on masochism. After all we live in a world of suffering and danger, and must eventually die. What can be more natural than to surrender ourselves to a god, submit to his will and accept his punishment? The founders of religions do not usually ask or want to be worshipped. They wish to lead their chosen people to salvation.

But the sadist's fantasies are gratified only when he inflicts pain. He is not able to surrender 'his will and person' to another being. 'Divine Love', says Dionysius the Areopagite, 'draws those whom it seizes beyond themselves: and this so greatly that they belong no longer to themselves but wholly to the object loved.' How can the sadist surrender when all his fantasies urge him to dominate? Only the masochist can surrender totally. Every mystic, all those saints who underwent a mystical conversion, had masochistic fantasies. St Paul on the road to Damascus, St John of the Cross, St Francis of Assisi, St Catherine of Genoa, St Theresa of Avila, the heroic Joan of Arc – all were masochists. St Francis 'loved beauty ... and shrank instinctively from contact with ugliness and disease. But something within ran counter to this temperamental bias, and sometimes conquered it. He would then associate with beggars, tend the leprous, perform impulsive acts of charity and self-humiliation.' Then came the moment when he saw and heard the painted image of Christ crucified speak to him, telling him to 'go, repair My House'. He obeyed unquestioningly, just

as Paul did after his vision. St Catherine was suddenly illu-
minated by a vision of her own misery and her faults, and
by the goodness of God. She cried, 'O Love, no more sins!'
'And her hatred of herself was more than she could endure.'

All such conversions have been preceded by a period of
mental conflict, between 'two discrepant ideals of life', a
struggle between pleasure and pain.

Of course many so-called mystical experiences and conversions are short-lived, without profound effects.

Gerry was at university, reading English literature. He
had few friends and often felt unhappy and restless. He
worried because he had no girlfriend, and because he masturbated with a fantasy of being tied up, blindfolded and
then beaten by a woman. He began to attend church
increasingly often. One day, during Evensong, he suddenly
saw the church windows lit up by a brilliant flame and,
beyond, a vast range of green hills. He felt a great sense of
peace, but that night he was unable to sleep. He left university and applied to join a religious order. During a six-month
probationary period he had to struggle increasingly hard to
ward off sexual fantasies and impulses to masturbate. Bouts
of overwhelming panic developed. Eventually he returned
to secular life, sadly aware that he had no deep religious
vocation.

Masochism must always have outweighed sadism in the
long run for civilization to have arisen. Although Freud at
first believed that masochism was derived from sadism – the
aggression initially directed against other people would turn
about and move against the self – he later came to believe
that masochism was a primary force (derived from the con-
troversial 'death instinct'), and that sadism arose secondarily
from it. It certainly seems feasible that the energy of masochistic fantasies can be directed away from the self on to an
enemy to combat a serious threat to the social group. The
masochist wishes to destroy the enemy for the sake of his

group. His satisfaction comes from this, not from any suffering he may cause the enemy. In fact many masochists feel sorry for a defeated enemy and subsequently offer help. Any pain or injury suffered by the masochist while aiding the fallen rival will doubly gratify his fantasies. The supreme masochist can endure torture, burning, all the agonies of martyrdom, so long as he continues to believe in his cause and his own heroic role. It is not difficult to see how masochistic fantasies can be harnessed for religious wars and persecutions.

The relationship between masochism and outward aggression is demonstrated by Albert. Albert had fantasies of being spreadeagled on the ground while native Indian women cut off and ate strips of his raw flesh. This fantasy had developed when he was ten, after reading a lurid 'cowboys and Indians' story. Since puberty Albert had masturbated regularly, thinking of this, but always with a sense of anxiety and guilt. Between 1943 and 1945 he fought against the Japanese in the Far East. During this time he occasionally masturbated, but only with the thought of making love to his wife. Six months after he returned home his prewar masochistic fantasy reappeared.

Sadistic fantasies are, from the very beginning, directed outside the self. The sadist who goes to war, directly satisfies his fantasies. His country or society is really of secondary importance. Cruelties in war for their own sake are always the work of people with sadistic fantasies. Such people rarely make good leaders, for they are too readily influenced, albeit unwittingly, by their fantasies. Whereas the masochistic leader has a clear idea of where he is going, the sadist's vision is less far-sighted and clear and he continually runs the risk of being sidetracked.

Every great hero, then, is masochistic at rock bottom. The sadist never wishes to be a hero. That Wagner appreciated this is brought out clearly in his operas: Tristan, Tannhäuser, Parsifal are all masochistic characters. Both Hitler's and Churchill's fantasies must have been masochistic. Hitler was dominated by Wagnerian images, by the 'glorious mystery of the dying hero'. He is said, in fact, to have sat through a hundred performances of *Tristan und Isolde*. Hitler probably hated the thought of physical torture or unkindness that involved him *personally*. His desire to be a hero to the German people must have stemmed from strong masochistic fantasies. He projected them on to the *Herrenvolk*, calling on them to endure terrible sufferings for the sake of a heroic future – the 'thousand-year Reich'. As success turned to failure he became increasingly depressed, and his heroic concept of himself had to be continually bolstered by an unrealistic sense of omnipotence. Ultimately he must have depended almost entirely on Eva Braun's adoration.

Much of the deliberately organized cruelty and suffering that occurs throughout the world comes from men and women with sadistic fantasies. It is often quite easy for people to disguise their sadistic needs, to act them out in the name of some idealistic cause: religion, nationalism, communism. Reality is partly taken over by fantasy, which then has an open door to the outside world. St Dominic leading the persecution of witches in the middle ages, the Inquisition in Spain and, on a lesser scale, schoolmasters beating their pupils, are all obvious examples. Many sadists need the reassuring security of an organization, within whose framework they can express their fantasies without anxiety. Any 'do-gooding' organization is likely to contain a fair quota of sadists who ultimately may come to dominate its policies. On the other hand, people with masochistic fantasies are more liable to be corrupted. The masochist's desire for ever greater powers, his need to be liked and admired, sometimes makes him susceptible to bribery and flattery. His sadistic colleague is too concerned with retaining control to allow himself to become beholden to another person.

During times of social upheaval, when the normal social controls break down and the distinguishing line between reality and fantasy becomes blurred, fantasy floodgates are liable to open, releasing sadistic and masochistic fantasies of terrifying dimensions. Thus Hitler and Stalin, although supremely masochistic in their need to lead their people to salvation, were able to use their people's fantasies to help them to gain control and retain power. The great purges of the 1930s in Russia, and the persecution of the Jews in Germany, harnessed mass sadistic and masochistic fantasies for the strength of the State; the sadist enjoyed beating up and terrifying the helpless victims, the masochist saw them as enemies of the State, proscribed by his hero and therefore to be eliminated.

Most of the leaders of the Third Reich, such as Hitler, Goering or Goebbels, behaved in ways characteristic of the masochist. It was the men and women behind the scenes – the anonymous Gestapo lieutenants, the SS men, the people who designed the gas ovens, the men who organized transport to the concentration camps – who were the sadists. Martin Bormann, Hitler's third deputy, was probably a sadist, for he was an obsessionally unobtrusive man with a hatred of being photographed. He was a back-room planner and, as sadists often are, was instinctively mistrusted by many of his colleagues. When the *Götterdämmerung* came for Hitler and Goebbels, he wanted no part in it. He left the bunker, for he had no masochistic death wish. It is difficult to say what Himmler's fantasies were. Though he may well have had a strong element of sadism, a masochistic side is suggested by the story that he was nearly sick on one occasion when he witnessed an extermination.

Men with strong sadistic fantasies do not easily lose their tempers or show deep emotions. If they can displace their fantasies on to work, and they have talent, they may succeed. Gerald, a property developer with fantasies of beating and torturing, gets considerable enjoyment from turning people out of their homes, and is attracted by property deals that are likely to lead to eviction.

But the sadist, lacking hero drive and hero worship, is not so likely to achieve success as the masochist of equivalent abilities. His colleagues may, sooner or later, sense the nature of his underlying fantasies and intuitively come to fear and distrust him.

Humour is a good indicator of the nature of fantasies. The witty masochist is rarely bitchy or nasty. The sadist, on the other hand, is often cruelly biting with his wit.

Sometimes the sadist becomes a 'Don Juan' – if he is not campaigning against the permissive society or encouraging the persecution of homosexuals. He may try compulsively to conquer women, not because he wants to feel loved, like the masochist, but rather from a need to dominate and humiliate, to feel reassuringly superior.

The sadist is an anxious person at heart, afraid lest his fantasies get out of control and show in real life. Severely sadistic fantasies almost invariably make a woman frigid and a man impotent, unless their partners are willing prostitutes or unwilling victims.

The apparently all-powerful head of any state will excite sexual fantasies in his or her subjects, regardless of the nature of the political system. This is particularly so in the United States, where the President wields such great power.

To be President of the United States probably entails being married: only one President, John Buchanan, has ever been a bachelor and it may be that Americans need to identify with a married couple in the White House for their peace of mind. The President's wife is automatically the First Lady, which is a very different role from, say, the wife of the British Prime Minister, whose charisma does not come anywhere near that of the Queen, who easily takes precedence over her in the hierarchy of female prestige. Not so with the First Lady; no one can touch her socially unless she abrogates her authority.

Of course, if a President and his Lady happen to be vastly favoured by the gods in terms of physique and good looks, they are more than usually likely to excite the envy of the less fortunate. The weaknesses of great men are the consolations of lesser mortals. Thus Jacqueline Kennedy, because of her personal beauty, charm and dashing individuality, was more vulnerable to the criticism of other envious and less talented women than, say, Mrs Woodrow Wilson or Mrs Calvin Coolidge. But on the whole the sexual fantasies woven around the President of the United States and his First Lady are similar to those excited by the leaders of any country.

Of course, if the First Lady suffers the loss of a husband by murder, like Mrs Kennedy or Mrs Lincoln, she will receive the pity and sympathy given to anyone who has sustained personal tragedy. Only the sadists will then continue to project their fantasies, often even more viciously because excited by the violence.

The sexual fantasies that are projected on to any monarch or president are enhanced by loose living and scandalous behaviour on their part. For instance, the story of the abdication of Edward VIII was taken up and elaborated by the western world as a twentieth-century example of the triumph of love and sexual passion. Whether Mrs Wallis and the erstwhile Prince of Wales were the most compatible of lovers was immaterial. The story of their marriage ranked, and still does in places, with *Romeo and Juliet* as one of the great love stories of the world.

Likewise, Jack Kennedy's and his younger brother Edward's supposed promiscuity enhanced their glamour in the eyes of their compatriots. Both men, as well as the redoubtable former Robert Kennedy, are symbols of potent masculinity to the women of America.

The Medical Profession

Many people are attracted into the medical profession under the influence of their fantasies. Of course, many doctors and nurses lead enjoyable, stimulating and socially acceptable lives. But the odds are that their professions are also satisfying some part of their fantasies. Indeed when medical students graduate it is revealing to see how the sadists and masochists intuitively choose different branches of medicine.

Both physicians and surgeons are likely to have masochistic fantasies. They play a heroic role, and are admired by nurses and patients alike. Yet not a few people regard surgeons as sadists, hacking and sawing for their own delight at least as much as for the good of the patient. Surgeons deal with cancer, perforations of the gut, and other painful, unpleasant conditions which many people are terrified of developing. Such fears often become displaced on to surgeons whose image then becomes that of a mutilator instead of a healer. But as well, the idea of lying helpless on the operating table while a surgeon opens and explores your insides readily rouses masochistic fantasies and transforms the good surgeon into a wicked rapist. In fact surgeons are on the whole more masochistic than other practitioners, and their often life-saving intervention is more dramatic and apparent. Although some of their techniques may seem to the uninitiated almost barbaric, and they carve up helpless unconscious people, they do all this in order to save them. Surgeons are the heroes of the medical profession (in the eyes of laymen) and earn more than other specialists. However, general practitioners are also widely admired and loved. Many of them require the reassurance of their patients' gratitude and devotion. Whereas surgeons tend to have 'passing affairs', general practitioners need the fruits of deeper emotional feeling, a love relationship, even if one way.

Psychiatrists and gynaecologists, by and large, are characterized by a mixture of sado-masochism, although the balance is still well on the side of masochism. Within the speciality of mental illness, psychoanalysts are probably the most sadistic, compelling their patients to twist and turn on the couch until they confess and conform. Yet their founder, Freud, was predominantly masochistic, destroying opposition and throwing those who disagreed with him out of the Psychoanalytic Society not for any sadistic pleasure but in order to ensure his own omnipotence.

Sadistic medical practitioners are most likely to become pathologists, radiologists and anaesthetists – doctors who are not emotionally close to their patients. They examine body fluids and tissues, measure the output of this or that organ, see the skull beneath the flesh, specialize in keeping a patient unconscious. They are the voyeurs of the medical profession, perhaps necrophiliacs of a sort. They are more controlled and inhibited than their clinical colleagues, more obsessional, unwilling to expose themselves in a clinical relationship.

Nurses on the whole are masochistic. They too are saviours of mankind, angels of mercy. What about the creator of the modern nursing profession, Florence Nightingale? Did she have masochistic fantasies? She certainly 'dreamed' a great deal before she finally left home to fulfil her ambition, and was disturbed by the content of her dreams. Perhaps she wanted both to be a heroine and to find and love a hero. But she refused all offers of marriage and went on to become a heroine in her own right. The anguish she suffered over her dreams and 'bad thoughts' is well documented in her diary:

Sometimes I think I will satisfy my passionate interest at all events, because that will at least secure me from the evil of dreaming . . . .

God has delivered me from the great offence and the constant murderer of all my thoughts.

I had no wish, no energy, I longed but for sleep . . . My enemy is too strong for me, everything has been tried . . . All, all is in vain.

Four long days of absolute slavery . . .

I lay in bed and called on God to save me.

Do these lines reveal masturbatory fantasies against which Florence Nightingale struggled, as the saints did? The answer of course detracts nothing from what she did and achieved for nursing.

Murderers

The majority of murders in Britain and the United States are committed in hot blood, during fits of jealousy and passion. The sexual psychopath who kills for sadistic pleasure is rare. Most killings of children and young adults during or after sexual assault occur as a result of the assailant's panic or desire to evade detection. But what of, say, the moors murders, or the poisoner, Graham Young, who cold-bloodedly killed several people? Crimes like these always provoke public fear and excitement, partly because they stimulate people's fantasies. Occasionally news of a particularly sadistic crime causes people to 'imitate' and act it out. Others, whose fantasies are equally stimulated, feel compelled by a sense of guilt to 'make a full confession' to the police. Many of these unfortunate confessors cannot distinguish clearly between fantasies and reality. Both the crimes of Graham Young and the moors murders led to furious demands for the reintroduction of the death penalty, suppression of pornography and harsher treatment for criminals generally and mad ones in particular. Yet there was no rational explanation for such demands and therefore it is worth taking a more detailed look at the moors murders.

The Moors Murders

Ian Brady, the man concerned in the case, was an outwardly meek and mild man. He had strong sadistic fantasies – when he was ten he was discovered torturing dogs – and had collected a large amount of sadistic pornography, including the works of the Marquis de Sade. Probably he masturbated while browsing through the books in his library, elaborating on the ideas he found there and incorporating them into his fantasies. All would probably have been well, as far as the rest of society was concerned, had he not met Myra Hindley. She was a masochist with a remarkably passive and suggestible personality, and she submitted herself totally to his fantasies. Once his fantasies were accepted and encouraged by a woman who loved him, the border between reality and fantasy was steadily and imperceptibly eroded for Brady. After the first victim was captured and killed, he must have felt increasingly omnipotent, controlled by his sadistic fantasies. Hindley's own masochistic fantasies were gratified because she identified herself in some measure with the victims. At the same time she surrendered herself totally to Brady, accepted him 'body and soul', and obeyed him without question. As in many sexual fantasies she became the torturer and the victim.

The capture and torture of each victim stimulated mutual sexual excitement. Copulation probably occurred only after the victim's death, and especially when the pair relived the awful scenes through their photographs and tape recordings. Or perhaps, as in other lust murders, the act of killing was satisfaction in itself.

Pornography was almost certainly not primarily responsible for Brady's behaviour. Indeed pornography for people like him – and there are not a few in our midst – can act more as a valve than a detonator. The moors murders illustrate how explosive antisocial forces may be liberated when a person with extreme sadistic fantasies is encouraged by a masochist. Myra Hindley was an example of extreme masochism: she was a hysterical personality, prone to dissociate (in a Jekyll and Hyde sense) under tension; in prison it cannot have been difficult for Lord Longford to convert her. But the dangers of such a *folie à deux* are as nothing compared to what can happen when large social groups are involved.

There are similarities between Brady and sadistic murderers in the United States like Charles Manson. Both are obsessive men, concerned with small details, socially uneasy and insecure. Brady had virtually no friends apart from Hindley. Manson had no friends, only followers. Unlike Brady, Manson was a drifter, unable to tolerate a steady, dull job. He became leader of a community of drop-outs, made up of people even more inadequate and unrealistic than himself. He developed theories and ideologies based on his sadistic fantasies, now fed by the admiration of his followers, and by his new found sense of power. As with Brady, fantasy became reality as Sharon Tate and four of her companions were murdered in horrifying ways. Without his followers Manson might well have remained harmless. Without Manson's influence his followers would probably have remained ineffective drop-outs.

Poisoning

Poisoning came suddenly to the British public's attention in 1973, with the trial of Graham Young. He had poisoned his father, sister and a schoolfriend when he was fourteen, had been sent to Broadmoor and released after nine years. He was now accused of poisoning at least four of his workmates, two of them fatally.

Poisoning always arouses public interest. Significantly it is the central feature of many myths and fairytales: the prince is turned into a frog, the maiden falls into a prolonged sleep, beauty is converted into ugliness. The poison is usually administered by a wicked stepmother, sister, dwarf, witch or wizard. The stricken victims remain helpless until released by love, nearly always of unsullied purity. Sometimes in these tales a love potion is substituted (accidentally or by design) for the poisoned draught; this causes the person who drinks it to become equally *hors de combat*, to fall hopelessly and helplessly in love, often with disastrous consequences.

Poisoning is linked in the public's subconscious mind with magical power, alchemy, transmutation, struggles between hate and love. And indeed poison is *par excellence* the favourite means of killing a hated rival, of satisfying a jealous lover. The method smacks of magic – the secret preparations, the outward friendliness of the poisoner towards his victim, the surreptitious placing of the crushed pearl in the drink, the arsenic in the cream cake.

Poisoning, in reality or fantasy, gratifies people with sadistic fantasies. The poisoner remains outwardly amiable as he offers hospitality to the unsuspecting victim. Like the arsonist his behaviour embodies both sexual and aggressive needs. Graham Young himself kept a meticulously detailed diary in which he recorded the events of every day: how his victims' hair fell out, the spreading paralysis of their limbs, the physical agony they suffered. As with arson, the sad fact is that once a poisoner, probably always a poisoner.

The Police and Firemen

And what of the fantasies of those who pursue murderers? Policemen are generally masochists, satisfied with being (heroic) father figures. A few people with sadistic fantasies may go into the uniformed branch (some traffic policemen, for instance, take an apparent delight in booking drivers), but they are more likely to gravitate to the CID. It must be difficult to be an efficient member of, say, the Vice Squad without having strong sadistic fantasies and voyeuristic tendencies. The satisfaction of being a policeman with sadistic fantasies, carrying out sadistic work, is that fantasy and work overlap, and the gratification of fantasies earns social approval. Of course the policeman's lot is a dangerous one, and he has to keep a tight rein on what is real and what is fantasy. But he has the advantage of being one of a team, and that reinforces reality. Small wonder, however, that the public love their local, friendly bobbies and often fear the CID.

Some people also fear motorcycle policemen. Leather-booted, dressed in black with goggles and helmets, they resemble figures in a sado-masochistic fantasy. The sight of one often arouses masochistic fantasies in women. Diana can have an orgasm only by imagining herself on the pillion of a stolen motorbike driven by her current boyfriend. Pursued by motorcycle policemen, they ride faster and faster until their bike skids off the road and crashes in a field. While the boyfriend lies dead beside her, the policemen take it in turn to beat her until she confesses to stealing the bike.

Firemen, like police constables, tend to be masochistic: they perform heroic feats like rushing into blazing buildings and rescuing helpless men, women and children or pets. But some firemen have sadistic fantasies and are fascinated by fire. Occasionally their fantasies break through and become reality; the fireman may then start his own fires. When arson breaks out in an area one of the first places the police visit is the local fire station.

The Armed Services

Officers of the armed services sometimes have even greater opportunities to gratify their fantasies than policemen. How their fantasies influence their lives depends to some extent on whether or not their country is at war. The soldier with strongly sadistic fantasies is attracted into the army in peacetime by thoughts of power and domination. The masochistic soldier rarely seeks power for its own sake. He wants to be a hero, saving his country, rescuing the flag, adding glory to it. 'Play up, play up and play the game!' is a masochistic battle cry. Massacring a thousand enemies before breakfast may be a joy to the sadist, but it means little to the masochist unless the victory results in his being acclaimed a hero.

In peacetime the chances of a soldier or sailor becoming a hero are limited. Masochists may therefore drop out of the armed forces and not push their way to the top. Those with sadistic fantasies, cautious, controlled, outwardly conforming and obedient, are more likely to remain in the service and to attain high command.

When war breaks out after many years of peace, officers with sadistic fantasies are therefore likely to be at the head of the services. But they lack the verve and dash of their masochistic colleagues. And they are all too likely to dither, because it takes a year or so of war before they fully accept the idea that it is respectable to kill ruthlessly and be 'sadistic' to the enemy. A masochist in charge (Churchill, for example) shows none of this dithering or reluctance to kill, because he does so to save his country.

Field Marshal Haig probably had sadistic fantasies. His behaviour during the First World War was typical of the sadist: unable to adjust to the new reality of war; utterly unimaginative, unpopular, obsessed with detail; almost, it seemed, engineering the massacres on the western front. Lloyd George regarded him as 'devoid of imagination'. Napoleon, Rommel, Nelson, Wellington were clearly men with strong masochistic fantasies. Each, in his way, enjoyed the company and admiration of women. All were ambitious, prepared to succeed or die, heroic and loved by their men. No sadist could have achieved what they did. Alexander the Great would never have conquered his empire had he not been a masochist. Indeed his sufferings during his travels would have put many a saint to shame. Lawrence of Arabia is perhaps the most obvious modern example of a leader with masochistic influences. Fantasy and reality are virtually inseparable in his book, *The Seven Pillars of Wisdom*. He portrayed himself as a hero, responsible for winning the war in the Middle East, the champion of the Arabs, and he described with relish the fearful privations and tortures that he said were inflicted on him.

There are many different facets to behaviour that is considered brave or cowardly. Neither the masochist nor the sadist can claim a monopoly of either. In the heat of struggle conscious controls may be diminished and consequently the influence of fantasy increased. The masochist is often recklessly brave as he hurls himself forward, blind to all dangers, intent on his heroic task. The sadist is sometimes a coward, considering discretion the better part of valour, wanting to avoid enduring pain himself. But on the other hand he may fight to the death, preferring this to the torture he knows will follow his capture.

The Acting Profession

Actors and actresses are in a position to act out their fantasies on the stage, though of course it is only those at the top, the heroes and heroines of the stage, who can do so. Perhaps all the really great players have well-balanced sado-masochistic fantasies, which allow them to undertake and portray a wide range of sadistic and masochistic characters. Shakespearean masochistic parts include Shylock, Antony, Caliban and Macbeth. Macbeth and Antony are good ex-

amples of masochistic men who fail in their bid for power. It
is natural for them to die bravely in the end.

Actors with predominantly sadistic fantasies may have the
luck to be cast for a truly sadistic role – such as Hamlet or
Iago. (Hamlet in fact is a good example. In so far as it is
justified to analyse dramatic characters, Hamlet has the hall-
mark of **a** sadist. He is an unheroic figure, without deep
passion, continually dithering, unable to act decisively,
stringing Ophelia along, causing his mother and uncle to
suffer anguish. His sadistic fantasies, stimulated by his desire
to kill his uncle and so avenge his father's death, frighten
him and bring him to a halt.) Most actors, however, have to
satisfy their sadistic fantasies indirectly by assisting a baddie,
or inverting fantasy by playing an out-and-out goodie, a
parody of anti-sadism.

Actors who play leading parts in horror films such as
Frankenstein or Dracula are usually masochistic. Their satisfaction derives from identifying with the sufferings of their
victims, which in turn makes their acting enjoyable and
convincing. Sadists are generally unable to identify closely
with events that are obviously unrealistic.

Viewers of sado-masochistic films and plays are in the
position of voyeurs, and are thus protected from direct emotional involvement. The enormous success of television
crime programmes on both sides of the Atlantic is in
large measure due to the way in which such programmes
appeal to people's fantasies. Some people will identify with
the villains as they are chased by good-looking policemen or
mercilessly grilled by hard-faced detectives, others with
the hunters. And many people with mild sadistic or masochistic fantasies will sympathize with both sides. The most
successful of these crime programmes, in fact, have a high
degree of ambiguity. Though they are sometimes praised
for being 'realistic', it is the fantasies they release that are
'real', rather than the events they portray.

Burglary and Shoplifting

Many crimes have sexual overtones. 'Amateur' burglars often break into homes not so much for what they can steal, but for the thrill of violating the privacy of a woman or married couple, of scattering underclothing across the floor, of defacing walls and floors with excreta and obscene graffiti. Shoplifting is the commonest offence committed by women (making up half their indictable offences), particularly by those in their fifties. Many of the objects stolen are cheap, and many of the shoplifters are relatively well-to-do. Behind their actions often lies repressed resentment, a sense of guilt, need for self-punishment, a desire to be loved 'at all costs'. Kleptomania sometimes alternates with masturbation.

Both are compulsive actions by women who feel unloved and unlovable. Stealing of this nature represents a childlike way of obtaining 'substitute love' and may be accompanied by frank sexual excitement. Masturbation reduces tension and the comparative urge to steal for a variable time. Sooner or later, particularly if the woman feels more lovable, masturbation may suffice.

A forty-year-old woman had had prolonged bouts of either masturbation or of stealing clothing and food since puberty. She married shortly after the death of her parents and lost all desire to do either. Another woman shoplifted food and cheap jewellery from the age of fourteen until menstruation began at seventeen. From then on she masturbated and lost the compulsion to steal. She came from an unhappy home and puberty gave her the confidence to leave home and seek more satisfying relationships.

The Legal Profession

Top barristers, like actors, are more likely to have masochistic than sadistic fantasies, particularly those who defend rather than appear for the prosecution. It is a common masochistic fantasy to imagine the loved one accused of some dreadful crime, or under sentence of death, saved at the last moment by the masochist's devotion and self-sacrifice.

Prosecuting barristers are perhaps more inclined to sadistic than masochistic fantasies, but much of the pleasure of their work comes from jousting with and defeating their colleagues, rather than achieving the conviction and therefore punishment of a villain. Of course if a defending barrister knew his client was guilty of some unpleasant crime, yet continued to defend him, he might well be satisfying his own sadistic fantasies in the process, even though he rationalized his action. A judge, on the other hand, is not engaged in battle. He umpires the match and punishes those found guilty. Barristers with sadistic fantasies are therefore most likely to apply to become judges.

Political Extremists

Causes that condone violence invariably attract people with strong sexual fantasies. People who plant bombs, or at any rate the leaders of, say, the IRA, who decide what is to be bombed, probably have masochistic fantasies. To them the act is a heroic one, carried out in the course of duty. They don't visualize the people who may be injured in the process (though they usually attempt to warn the authorities in time to clear the area). If they do see pictures of dead and wounded bystanders they often feel pity and remorse for them. One of the 'bombers' in a recent bomb trial in the UK wept and expressed anguish at the physical pain and suffering that had resulted. Thus the Price sisters, who were involved in the Old Bailey bomb explosion in London in March 1973, are probably masochistic (their self-imposed starvation and at the time therefore inevitable forced feeding in prison is in keeping with masochism).

But for the sadist a place like Ireland, where he can actually gratify his fantasies of killing and torturing, may offer delightful opportunities. The fantasies of bomb hoaxers, like obscene telephone callers, are always strongly sadistic; they obtain great pleasure in fantasizing the suffering and terror resulting from their bombs. In the manner of an arsonist they will often compulsively watch the evacuation of a building threatened by their telephone bomb warning. Some of these hoaxers masturbate at the scene, others while making the call.

Espionage

People who spy for their countries are of course very different from the glamorous, womanizing James Bond image. Many of them are rather lonely, unhappy people, with sadistic fantasies that, to some extent, they can act out. They carry guns, interrogate people, sometimes even torture them – and all in the name of their country or ideal. The very nature of most intelligence work, sifting through reports, closely scrutinizing statements and people's behaviour, requires an obsessional nature and, of course, an anonymous, retiring personality.

Kim Philby, the 'third man' in the Burgess–Maclean affair and one of the most successful spies of all time, seems to have exhibited these characteristics *par excellence*. Those who knew him describe him as 'gentle and kind', qualities that are the hallmarks of the man with sadistic fantasies. Although a good conversationalist at the dinner table, Philby had a retiring personality. He never spoke of his personal feelings and shrank away when other people tried to tell him about theirs. A domineering father, whom he always feared and respected, may well have contributed to the formation of his fantasies and his lifelong stammer. Philby never did anything rashly and all his actions were considered. Even when the full extent of his activities began to be appreciated by the British authorities he organized his escape as coolly as he had engineered the disappearance of Burgess and Maclean when they were about to be arrested.

Philby also possessed a quality that many sadistic people have, the ability to laugh inwardly when outwitting others. Both masochistic and sadistic people may return to the scene of their crime (the masochist out of compulsion to be caught and punished, the sadist out of a desire to gloat). If the sadist is caught the blow to his ego is profound. But in Philby's case his intelligence was such that he invariably came out on top. As correspondent for *The Times* during the Spanish civil war he won several awards, both from professional journalist bodies and from General Franco, for his pro-fascist articles, written at a time when he was already a committed communist. After the Burgess–Maclean affair became public knowledge and he was openly accused in the House of Commons of being the 'third man', he still dared to return home from a holiday in Spain and successfully face a gruelling three-day secret tribunal enquiry into his past life. He emerged with his 'honour' untarnished, and the Secret Service continued to employ him.

Burgess and Maclean, on the other hand, were both intensely masochistic, and it is astonishing that they survived for so long as spies. Whereas Philby despised the 'Old Boy network' and secretly laughed at many of his colleagues, Burgess and Maclean were a guilt-ridden couple, tormented by the duality of their existence. Maclean drank heavily, and towards the end incessantly, and this habit led him into many compromising situations. When drunk his homosexual side emerged, he became indiscreet and sometimes spoke openly about his treacherous activities. Philby cleverly steered him into social circles where people did not notice, or, if they did, think anything of his behaviour.

Burgess was also an alcoholic, although he kept a tighter rein on his drinking than Maclean. He was also an un-ashamed homosexual who, from his Cambridge days, liked shocking people. All his life he enjoyed drunken all-night orgies (a very masochistic life style). Although predomi-nantly a masochist, he may well have possessed a sadistic component, which was used by Philby. It was Burgess who, on Philby's instructions, first blackmailed Maclean into becoming a spy, and who maintained pressure on Maclean whenever he showed signs of wavering. Despite his chaotic life he carefully kept all his boyfriends' love letters (several of them were quite prominent people) in labelled bundles.

Sport and Pastimes

Situations like Philby's are not, of course, available to most people in their everyday lives and they therefore need to find other outlets for their fantasies. Very often people find outlets in sports and games, as participant, spectator, or both. The masochistic hero-worship of sportsmen, which can reach ludicrous proportions, is an interesting example of how sexual fantasies can be diverted into apparently non-sexual activities. Many men have fantasies of scoring twenty goals against an opposing team, to the admiration of the millions. And many women are excited by the sight of a sports hero on the television. Indeed the games people enjoy watching and playing, at both the professional and amateur level, are often an indication of their predominant sexual fantasies.

Members of a team, say football or rugby, are likely to be masochistic. Each plays for the honour of the team, but each also aims to be the team hero. In a brilliant soccer team there will be eleven masochistic players, each striving to outshine his team mates, yet all working together as one.

The same applies to baseball and cricket, with the possible exception of certain great opening batsmen. These people, whose task it is to lay the foundation for a good score and demoralize and tire their opponents, need to be cautious, obsessive, unheeding of the crowd, who may be booing and giving them a slow handclap, conscious only of the ball and the bowlers as *objects* to be punished. Only masochists are aware of their opponents as individuals; sadists seem to depersonalize their opponents.

Top-class boxers like Mohammed Ali are masochists, able to see their opponents as individuals. Ali increases his awareness of an opponent by insults before the fight (which also of course serves to upset the opponent). Most second-rate professional boxers are simply sadists, incapable of ever becoming heroes.

Professional players with sadistic fantasies are particularly likely to be encountered in pastimes like archery, bridge or chess. Top-class bridge is *par excellence* a sadistic game, depending on a close relationship between two people. Masochism and a desire to be heroic would be a disadvantage here. Bridge players need to have a good memory and a trusting, understanding, yet aggressive relationship with their partners. There are many fine individual bridge champions but there are no heroes at the table. There, opponents exist purely as objects to be defeated and no true hero can really abide an equal partnership.

Chess at the professional level differs fundamentally from bridge in that it is an individualistic, not a partnership, game. There are no excuses for losing at chess, as there are in bridge – no luck of the cards, no partner to blame, no partnership misunderstanding. There is only oneself. Many second-rate tournament chess-players are sadistic and unaware of their opponents except as 'objects'. The best grandmasters, however, are likely to be masochistic, since in order to win at chess at that level considerable knowledge and awareness of one's opponent, his strengths and weaknesses, are required. Alekhine who, apart from two years, held the world championship from 1927 to his death in 1946, was an out-and-out masochist who fought a lifelong struggle against alcohol and chain-smoking. It is still difficult to see what Bobby Fischer's fantasies are. His Mohammed Ali style of pre-play insults is a masochistic characteristic and suggests that he has a good understanding of his opponent's psychology. On the other hand he leads a lonely, apparently misogynous and unheroic life. Having won the chess world championship, the masochist is far more likely than the sadist to take risks in his play and increase his chances of defeat, unlike Fischer so far.

The Effect of Fantasies on the Sexual Partner

It is relatively easy to understand how fantasies can be displaced and channelled into work in an acceptable way. But alas! by no means everyone is able to find a job that will use his abilities and fulfil his needs. And in any case many people's fantasies are too strong to be safely and effectively transposed. They remain below the surface, all too often causing some form of sexual or psychological disturbance. Impotence, frigidity, premature ejaculation and related problems are fairly common in our society; in only a tiny number of cases is the problem a physical one. Ninety-nine times out of a hundred sexual problems are caused by a person's inability to associate his or her sexual fantasies with his or her partner.

Men have always felt threatened sexually by women. A

man has to *prove* his potency with a woman. A woman merely has to lie or kneel down and, at the worst, 'close her eyes and think of England'. A man needs an erect penis to make love to a woman and no woman thinks much of her man as a lover if he can never manage an erection with her at the appropriate time. What is more she will begin to feel increasingly frustrated, rejected and unattractive. And those feelings will be aggravated by apologies, explanations and excuses that only add insult to injury – that he was successful in the past with another woman, or that he has erections at the 'wrong time'.

A woman in this situation may rush out and have an affair with the first willing male she can find, to prove to herself that she is still sexually attractive. If she subsequently taunts her man and boasts of this episode, he may become so angry that his sexual anxiety is overcome and he suddenly becomes potent. But more often such behaviour only adds jealousy to her lover's sense of inadequacy and impotence.

Alternatively, a woman may accept her partner's impotence and satisfy her unrequited sexual needs by masturbating. She may 'split' him into two parts, good and bad, idealizing the desexualized 'good' part and secretly criticizing and despising the 'bad' failed lover. Less desirable forms of compensation include psychosomatic illness, alcoholism, gambling and even breeding miniature poodles.

In almost every case of premature ejaculation and sexual failure the man is impotent with the woman because he fears her or, to be more exact, fears intercourse with her. He may fear all women and be inadequate with them all, or only one particular woman. He may be able to perform like a hero with a 'lower-class girl', barmaid, prostitute or woman of another race, yet be only able to hang his penis in shame before his beautiful wife. A man may go to considerable lengths to persuade his fiancée, out of fear, that they should not have intercourse before marriage, while he does not scruple to seduce his mother's housekeeper. If his fiancée goes along with his wishes all will be well, for during the engagement her loved one's penis, effectively sheltered, will respond to her presence. Both man and woman will be comforted and reassured.

Occasionally the usual social class potency differential is reversed. Herbert, a bus driver, impotent with his (socially equal) wife, discovered that he could copulate with the nurse who had looked after him in hospital. Eve, a shipping magnate's wife, was sexually satisfied by a taxi driver she picked up, who was impotent with his own wife. The bus driver was jealous, without foundation, of his wife, but enjoyed his friends' admiration of her. The taxi driver idealized his wife and repeatedly told her she was beautiful and that he loved her.

Idealization and Envy

Both males and females, particularly during adolescence, are liable to idealize a person of the opposite sex. To idealize someone (such as when you fall in love) is to see him or her as a superior being, free from defects. The idealizer feels himself to be in an inferior position, almost ashamed of attracting the other's attention. The ideal is to some extent desexualized, so that even though the person is physically attracted to someone the thought of sexual contact, especially at first, seems to be a minor matter, perhaps even shocking. Some people, such as the taxi driver referred to above, find it difficult to break out of what can become a vicious circle.

Idealization is a way of diminishing anxiety. Anyone who over-idealizes another person, or even an institution, lacks confidence in himself and in his own individual worth as a member of society. This is a characteristic feature of many of the people who cling fervently to a political group or association, an old school tie, a club, regiment and so on. The Queen is often idealized, especially by women, but also by those whose vocations are applauded by society, although not necessarily well rewarded – they identify with the Queen's virtuous dedication. She is also thought of as pure and good, and men who adore her (often homosexuals who, for the same reasons, are attracted to mariolatry) make her sexless. Few, apart from the most rabid republican, would think of making love to the Queen, although Pepys, it is true, went to bed 'sporting in my fancy with the Queen'. But because she is put on a pedestal it is the unlucky lot of some other members of the royal family to compensate for this by being considered weaker and wickeder than the rest of us.

Of course the privileged – and the successful – have always been the target of malicious envy. To some men Prince Philip symbolizes power and potency, and to some women he is the perfect man – handsome, successful, authoritarian, protective. But the fact that he is married to the Queen can arouse opposing emotions. Those who look up to the Queen see him as a rival, threatening to sexualize their ideal. Yet if he openly took a mistress and thus in a way preserved the purity of the Queen, so much conflicting passion would be publicly released that inevitably the image of the Queen herself would become tarnished.

The same spectrum of attitudes was apparent during the engagement of Princess Anne and Mark Phillips. A vast array of books, magazines and newspaper space was given over to this couple and their activities. Much of the writing, while idealizing Anne as the pure, beautiful, Olympic show-jumping princess, was hostile and derogatory to Captain Phillips. Considerable emphasis was laid on his (minor) car accident and on the fact that his father was a director of a sausage-making company. The historical fear of royalty 'tainting its blood' by marrying commoners, which is still strong, arises out of the discrepancy in people's minds between the ideal and the reality. For behind the outward adoration of all idealizers lurks their lack of self-confidence, releasing fear and angry indignation at the slightest hint of criticism or disturbing news of the ideal. The sensed threat to the idealizer's inner security and peace of mind may be great enough to evoke an extreme and outwardly absurd reaction.

Of course, all of us have ideals. Many of our most socially laudable attributes have evolved through countless generations of idealization. Poetry, painting, architecture, all forms of art rely to some extent on idealization, on suppressed and displaced sexual instincts and fantasies. So civilizations arise through the innate ability of their peoples to idealize.

And what happens when people cease to idealize an 'object'? Beauty and truth crack and crumble, and previously hidden fears and unacceptable feelings and fantasies are exposed. Creation gives way to destruction. Gods and goddesses are abandoned. Empires once glorified are ridiculed. Love turns to hatred. Sometimes the change is permanent, sometimes feelings oscillate between the two extremes.

This process is often seen today in outbreaks of mass hysteria. Young girls idealize a top-of-the-charts pop singer. They see him as beautiful, heroic, talented, beyond compare. They extol his virtues and vie with one another for extravagant superlatives. Then comes the long-awaited public appearance of the hero. Excitement mounts among the audience. Rhythmic music, clapping, screams, heat, help to increase tension and reduce individual consciousness and self-control. At the sight of their idol the teenagers are psychologically overwhelmed. They surge forward, screaming, hearts racing, breathless, some almost fainting, wanting to seize, devour, possess him. Like women in a Dionysian rite they long to tear the godlike pop star to pieces, and would do so if they were unrestrained. But the last thing any of them really wants is to sleep with him unless accompanied by a heap of their friends. The fears and aggression that lie beneath all idealization suddenly come to the surface and dominate the girls' behaviour as their self-consciousness diminishes and they become part of the crowd. 'Civilized', inhibited public behaviour gives way to childlike, primitive reactions. They want to devour, not to love or idealize, their hero. Afterwards some are shocked and disturbed by the way they behaved, by what they can recall of their feelings at the time. Others are elated, having found a release from their inhibitions.

Young men are equally carried away by a rock star's appearance, or by the fortunes of the sports teams they support. When their favourites are defeated they hurl themselves in destructive fury upon the supporters of the opposing team. Their idealization may hide fears of impotence and failure, a lack of self-assurance. When their team loses idealization is temporarily shattered, and under the hypnotic influence of the crowd anger and destructiveness run riot. Even when their team wins the young supporters may riot, identifying themselves with their heroes, wanting to emulate their victory.

Although self-control usually increases with age, no one can be sure of not being caught up in a movement of mass hysteria. When large groups of people become emotionally, intellectually or sexually frustrated, horrifying results may occur from fantasies becoming reality, as witness the witch-hunts examined in Chapter 6.

We have so far looked at many of the common (and uncommon) fantasies that people have, the various ways in which we cope with them and how they influence us. To understand more about how we have them and how deeply embedded in our make-up they are, we must look back to our childhood and see how they are formed.

3 The Development of Sex and Sexual Fantasies

The dreamcrossed twilight between birth and dying (Bless
me father) though I do not wish to wish these things. . . .
T.S.Eliot

Most of us have little difficulty in accepting the fact that
physically we are male or female. It is when we consider
our psychological make-up, our degree of masculinity and
femininity, that doubts and fears arise.

Some authorities believe that infants are psychosexually
undifferentiated at birth, and that they only gradually learn
their sexual genders. The first two or three years are considered the most important in this respect. Any attempt to
change a person's sexual role after the age of three or four
is looked upon as psychologically hazardous. It certainly
seems to be the general rule that any child who is labelled
and brought up in the wrong sex opts to remain there.
(Think of the palaver and expense, not to mention the
embarrassment, of changing.) But cases are recorded of such
people, usually at puberty, choosing to reassign themselves
to their proper biological sex and adapting successfully to the
change. For this to happen a stable personality is obviously
extremely important.

Boys whose sex is not ambiguous are occasionally dressed

and brought up as girls during their childhood – Elizabeth Barrett Browning's son, Penini, for instance. Some of these change 'almost overnight' at puberty into heterosexual men. But others are content to remain 'neuter' pseudo-females, or compromise by becoming homosexual males. However recent evidence suggests that the idea of our being psychosexually undifferentiated at birth is wrong and that most of us are predisposed to one sex or the other. Sex differences exist from an early age, and of course parents continually reinforce behaviour that they consider to be sex appropriate. Inevitably parents respond differently to a boy or girl, however much they may try not to, not only because of the way they perceive the child, but also because of subtle differences in the child's response.

No one description of what constitutes male or female human behaviour and temperament will ever be universally acceptable. Even our present-day concepts are unlikely to endure for more than a decade or so. A woman from another culture, be it Chinese, American or Italian, behaves very differently from an Englishwoman. And the very word 'Englishwoman' is misleading, for the characteristic behaviour of one social class often differs from that of another. The working-class woman in the West is still dominated by her man; her main function is to look after him and raise his children. Women of the upper social and economic classes are more likely to demand equality with men and when they have children, they increasingly expect their husbands to share the responsibilities and ties of family life, and to continue outside interests.

The ideal Victorian wife was pictured as the loving custodian of her family, the 'angel in the house', always ready to give of herself, gentle, kind, understanding and unassuming. Her male equivalent was the hardworking, reliable husband and father. But unlike his wife the man was recognized as having sexual appetites that sometimes got out of control. Today many of us still associate masculinity with aggression, femininity with passivity and submissiveness, particularly in the field of sexual behaviour. Women are envisaged as sensitive, warm, protective, kindly and intuitive, characteristics that stem partly from our family structure and from our length of childhood dependence. But these ideas also reflect basic physical differences between men and women: male strength; the fact that only women can bear children; that only a man can possess a penis.

Men in general think of sex in terms of a man pushing his penis into a woman, and not of a woman pushing herself on to the penis or sucking it into herself. But of course there is no direct connection between sexual and non-sexual aggressiveness. In fact the opposite may be true. Harold, a highly successful, ruthless businessman – whose sex fantasies are masochistic, in keeping with his temperament – is continually seeking out sexually active, dominating women, and satisfying his fantasy needs by playing the passive role. And many a dynamic businesswoman is sexually passive and masochistic, longing to be overwhelmed by an heroic sex fiend. It is difficult to imagine anyone being wholly 'masculine' or completely 'feminine'. Such a person would be a caricature of present-day prejudices and ideals.

Sadistic and masochistic fantasies are present in both men and women, although extremes of sadism are largely a male prerogative. This fact is probably related to constitutional differences, since the rudiments of fantasies develop in the first three or four years of life. Men and women also tend to differ in the ways their adult sexual fantasies manifest themselves after puberty. Most adolescent boys develop strong sex drives at puberty, or even a year or so before, and fantasies surge into consciousness and demand satisfaction, usually through masturbation. The majority of men masturbate regularly until they find a partner for coitus. The five per cent or so who don't either have a low sex drive or develop late emotionally, and during adolescence devote their time and energies to academic pursuits. But sooner or later, and particularly when such men reach college or begin a job, emotional forces begin to predominate over purely intellectual activities and their fantasies change.

Many women, on the other hand, don't become aware of their sexual fantasies until years after adolescence. Ambition and the drive to succeed at work, avoidance of deep emotional relationships, hero worship of an unattainable or sexually non-threatening man, any of these may help to preserve women from becoming conscious of and pressurized by sexual fantasies. Women's fantasies often only appear after sexual arousal, and then centre on the partner. Most men, in contrast, have to deal with their sexual fantasies in a vacuum. In fact, it may be difficult for them to link up their fantasies with their partners later.

Infantile and Childhood Sexuality

From a psychosexual point of view it is impossible to talk of masculinity and femininity with any real meaning. Such terms merely signify current concepts of the role of each sex within society. We are all in some measure bisexual. Most of us oscillate between aggressive and passive sexual behaviour, and it is important to remember this in discussing fantasies. Much of our ambiguity derives from childhood and the various attitudes children have towards their parents and, to a lesser extent, to their siblings.

It was Freud who first put forward the idea of infantile sexuality to describe a child's complex love and hatred for his parents and the way in which he derives special pleasure from stimulation of certain areas of his body. Freud pointed out that the instinctive incest between children and parents, and vice versa (Oedipus complex), which occasionally culmi-nates in sexual intercourse, is natural. It is paradoxical that Freud, a man lacking in sexual drive (at the age of forty-one he wrote to a friend that his sexual life was over and done with), should have been regarded for so long as something of a sex monster.

The concepts of infantile and childhood sexuality need to be distinguished from adult, genital sexuality. From the earliest years great pleasure is experienced when various parts of the body are stimulated by stroking or pressure, particularly the genital areas. Babies play with their genitals from around four to five months, boys more than girls (not unnaturally, since a penis is a more obvious toy). Erection of the penis can occur from birth onwards. This is not a fore-taste of superhuman virility, but a reflex spinal cord response to a full rectum. Indeed it is misleading to label such beha-viour 'sexual' or to speak of 'infantile masturbation', thereby implying that the young child experiences the same sexual hunger and appetite as the adult.

Sex play and self-stimulation during early childhood are not only pleasurable but comforting to a child. From two or three years onwards sexual activities begin to be directed towards other people. Motives include curiosity, sensual pleasure and excitement, and, particularly among older children, an instinctive need to relate to another person. Sex play is a 'normal' activity throughout childhood, although it may be driven underground because of parental disapproval.

Young children respond with pleasure to the stimulation of virtually any part of their bodies. Freud noted the exis-tence of certain erotogenic or dominant pleasure zones, which gradually shift in dominance as the child develops: from mouth to anus to genitals. He believed that in the normal course of growing up these first erotogenic zones lost their sensual qualities, so that sexual pleasure eventually became confined to the genital area. He described childhood sexuality as 'polymorphous perverse', meaning that all erotic potentialities were explored by the child, by means of his own body, through the bodies of others, directly or at a distance, by touching and being touched, watching and listening.

It is man's relatively prolonged childhood, and particularly the close mother–child relationship that exists in all mammals (you'll never, for this reason, find a homosexual or fetishist beetle; the sexual patterns of insects are stereotyped and fixed from birth), plus the necessity for the child to repress much of his 'infantile sexuality', that shapes his adult sexual behaviour and needs and creates the sexual problems that appear to be unique to mankind. It is from the child's long-drawn-out social experiences and encounters that his sexual fantasies and adult problems arise.

An infant is probably incapable of separating 'I' from 'not I'. He responds to hunger and discomfort, or gratification of his needs, at first through his reflexes, then with increasing awareness as the boundaries of his identity become more clearly perceived, as the people and objects necessary to him are recognized. Satisfaction of his hunger and thirst, of the wish to be hugged and rocked and fondled, to be warm and comfortable, is followed by signs of pleasure and relaxation, dissatisfaction by anxiety and rage. But what can an infant or young child do if his needs are unmet, apparently ignored? No doubt he feels destructive, much as adults do when frustrated. But sooner or later, if his anger and misery and anxiety are unassuaged, the child is forced back on to his own resources, on to self-gratification.

Childhood masturbation is pleasurable and relaxing. The unhappy child comes increasingly to rely on self-stimulation to satisfy his frustrated needs. Of course every child is unhappy and angry on occasions, and may use masturbation at such times. But the constantly unhappy child tends to use masturbation as a substitute for an unsatisfactory relationship. Masturbation now becomes the main outlet for his loneliness, anger and sense of deprivation. He discovers that through his fantasies he is virtually omnipotent, that he can control and provide for himself what he cannot obtain in real life. And at the same time he recreates for himself the person for whom he longs and whose love he craves. Masturbation is such a child's way of dealing with his unhappiness and unsatisfactory relationships, a means of taking revenge, of dealing out retribution, of relieving guilt, of relaxation, pleasure and power. Through his fantasies he becomes the master of his world, is transformed from a helpless being into an all-powerful emperor. All his sensual and emotional needs that have been searching for an object now become displaced on to masturbation and its fantasies.

Gradually, children who feel compelled to bottle up their anger and other strong emotions in order to gain love become polite, tidy, inhibited and self-controlled, yet seething with fearful sadistic fantasies. Other children – perhaps more gratified, or constitutionally different – experience such guilt over their sadistic urges that they displace their anger against themselves, and develop masochistic fantasies. Once elaborated, these fantasies become ever more firmly entrenched and associated with masturbation. All kinds of objects, apart from people, may now become associated with a child's masturbation fantasies. As a result, sexual fetishism may arise later, a problem that is discussed in Chapters 5 and 7.

All early masturbatory fantasies are probably incestuous, involving those members of the child's family who have most to do with him. But with time other non-incestuous objects become increasingly important. Guilt often follows masturbation, not unnaturally in view of the nature of fantasies and their origins. At puberty fantasies and masturbation are occasionally suppressed out of guilt and fear, totally or partly, or made to function separately, distorted and disguised. Ideally men and women must eventually accept their fantasies and allow them access to the 'real' world, controlled through a sexual partnership.

Freud thought of adult sexuality as being, in one sense, an 'unnatural tyranny' developing out of a repression of childhood sexuality. Of course any civilization is bound to inhibit and distort sexual needs and behaviour. Some degree of discontent with our sexual lives is probably inevitable at some time. Yet a large amount of the lovemaking of two adults, culminating in orgasm, is a fusion of adult and childhood sexuality. Many lovers need to flow backwards in time, back to their childhood, their time of innocence and shame, of destructive rage and guilt, to feel again what they experienced in childhood.

Consider William, able to copulate only when he imagines himself an angry, struggling, helpless child, held at arm's length by a huge, bulging woman. 'She was a bitch, my mother,' he explained. 'She always kept me hungry.' And yet to others his mother seems a kindly soul whose only vice is over-indulging William. He is attracted to plump 'vulgar' barmaids and has had affairs with several, but he believes that he is too complex and difficult a character for marriage. He is successful and ambitious in his work, yet he is for ever feeling miserable, a failure and a sham. 'Something is missing in my life,' he said. 'I have never been whole. If only I could love and be loved.'

The main reason why prostitutes continue to flourish today is that they provide facilities for those aspects of childhood sexuality that men crave through their fantasies, and that they cannot or dare not experience at home except through masturbation.

Adult Sexuality

What is adult or genital sexuality? Technically it means the ability of either sex to experience genital orgasm, whether or not through genital stimulation, alone or with one or more partners. For this to happen a person must be sexually excited and tense. It is easy enough to describe the *feeling* of sexual excitement. What generates it is more difficult to define.

No man can make love to his partner, however beautiful, graceful and well-rounded, unless he can colour and distort her in his fantasy mirror, or (alas!) cover her up and go off with his fantasy. A woman can make love without sexual excitement, although sooner or later suppressed fantasies are liable to break through and cause psychological trouble.

Both childhood and adult sexuality require a drive, searching for sexual pleasure. And drive needs an object of pursuit, living or inanimate, around which fantasies may be woven. Adult sexual drive, performance and orgasm depend upon adequate levels of circulating sex hormones and an intact nervous system. A balanced concentration of different chemicals that act as neurotransmitting substances in the brain is also essential. Penile and clitoral erections then occur during sexual excitement, vaginal secretions flow and there are widespread changes throughout the body. Orgasm coincides with the climax of sexual tension, resulting (usually) in the man ejaculating semen.

Strength of sexual drive probably depends on a number of components. There is enormous individual variation. Some people, both male and female, seem to possess little or no drive, and pass their lives unperturbed by sexual frustrations and disturbances. They neither sow nor reap in any field. Such men and women marry mainly from a wish for children and security. It is a strange fact that some women with an apparently low sex drive have a compulsion to produce large families. Most of their pleasure derives from the experience of childbirth, which is like a gigantic orgasm to them and the baby is the aim and end-product of intercourse. (Not all women who voluntarily have large families are lacking in sex drive, of course. There are obviously many other reasons for wanting children.)

Men with a low sex drive make faithful, trustworthy, dull husbands, content to live quietly, well within the limits of their capability, devoted family men. But some 'neuters', of both sexes, although apparently lacking sex drive, may be ambitious and successful in other aspects of life. William Pitt the Younger, for instance, was considered by his contemporaries to be a neuter. A successful political life is particularly likely to draw people's attention to the absence of sexual life and cause speculation.

Some people have fierce and violent sexual drives that need to be displaced and directed into other outlets: work, religion, politics, art, travel, exploration. Every fanatic, every saint and most geniuses have probably had strong sexual drives that they have diverted into other channels after a long, hard struggle.

The Mechanics of Sex

Before we move once more into the world of fantasies and how they affect our lives, it is worth noting the mechanics of sex and how this interacts with fantasies.

A two-way feedback system exists between the brain and the genitals. Erection depends fundamentally upon a spinal reflex arc that can be inhibited or enhanced by the brain. Erection has a positive feedback effect on fantasy activity and diminishes anxiety. Provided fantasy thinking is not interrupted or upset, erection is maintained and sexual excitement grows until orgasm is reached. The role of this two-way feedback system can be seen in the case of Stephen.

Stephen had been sexually impotent with his wife for almost ten years, although potent with other women. He then fractured his spine and was paralysed below the waist.

As a result the spinal cord pathway between his brain and the reflex arc serving erection of his penis was severed. His penis now became erect by reflex when the skin around his genitals was touched. He felt nothing, and no fantasies accompanied erection and intercourse. His wife was now able to have intercourse with him, for the sexual inhibitions originating in his brain were not able to reach and influence his lower spinal centres.

The reactions of different parts of the body during sexual excitement have been recorded by Kinsey, and more recently by Masters and Johnson. Pulse and blood-pressure rise and reach a sudden peak at orgasm, then return quickly to their pre-excitement levels. Respiration increases and becomes deeper and gasping at orgasm. Salivary secretion alters and is often profuse before orgasm. As orgasm approaches a person's awareness of what is going on round him, in fact of all sensation except sexual, diminishes and may be momentarily lost during orgasm — injuries that would normally cause considerable pain sometimes go unfelt until after orgasm. The face becomes contorted and the mouth opens and gasps for air. Eyes screw up, or if open stare blankly into the distance. During both masturbation and sexual intercourse men and women become, just before and during orgasm, totally involved and alone with their fantasies. Guilt and depression all too often follow orgasm, the consequence of unrelieved sexual fantasies. But in a loving relationship each partner is absolved of guilt. Love and desire, instead of being slaked, are fed by one another's fantasies.

Men and women both take about the same time to reach orgasm by masturbation. If a woman is already sexually aroused when intercourse begins, she is usually able to reach orgasm just as quickly as her mate. But in practice most people like, and need, to prolong intercourse and love-making.

Just before orgasm, tension reaches a peak. This is then

suddenly released in a series of convulsions and muscular spasms. The contractions may be localized only, or they may affect the entire body, and last from seconds to minutes. Some people find these spasms extremely painful and unpleasant, particularly during masturbation. Vaginal spasms during orgasm are strong and provide a source of intense pleasure to the man. The intensity of a woman's orgasm is related to the number of spasms, although other factors, particularly psychological ones, also exert a strong influence. Orgasm is usually, but by no means always, followed by reduction or cessation of sexual hunger and appetite. Sexual fantasies then stop abruptly. But appetite, particularly in women, may remain unassuaged; some women are capable of several orgasms a minute for twenty minutes or more, although the psychological satisfaction of this is limited. Most men take at least fifteen minutes, often longer, after orgasm and emission to regain erection, even if sexual appetite returns sooner.

Adult sexual drive is directed at someone or something. The majority of us are heterosexual – that is, we are attracted to the opposite sex. Most people are capable of homosexual behaviour but only about four per cent of either sex have predominantly homosexual interests. Some men are aroused only by the sight and feel of a mackintosh or plastic sheet, by women's clothes, hair, high-heeled shoes, leather boots and so on. Some are attracted only to children, a few to dead and unconscious women. Others need to indulge in sadistic or masochistic acts. The range of objects and situations that at one time or another has aroused man's passions is vast.

Early Sexual Development

The fact that sexual excitement is sometimes associated with unusual objects and situations might be related to events and encounters in early childhood, well before the age of five. There is no reason to doubt that sexual deviations are learned, even if there must be individual predispositions. Although it may be difficult for many of us to comprehend how a sardine tin can become an object of sexual delight, it is virtually impossible to conceive of such a passion as being inherited from one's parents. Yet why should one person become deviant and not another? Why should virtually all fetishists be male? It is simply evading the problem to attribute all deviations to 'castration anxiety', however symbolic the term. (There must in fact be far more danger of the deviant damaging his penis in the sardine tin.)

The source of deviation probably starts *in utero*, before birth. Faults in the areas of the brain concerned with sexual functions and behaviour, from genetic or environmental causes, result in the child being 'predisposed' in the first few years, so that learning, or imprinting, goes awry. Learning derives at first largely from a child's mother, since in our society the mother usually has most contact with children. Quite apart from those neurotic mothers who dress their sons in frilly skirts and generally try to emasculate them, it is common sense to suppose that boys, by and large, have more difficulty in developing a sense of identity than girls. Mother's body and behaviour make identification, and therefore identity, relatively easy for girls. A boy has to resist being swamped by female identification, and perhaps it is in the process of this early struggle that deviation occurs. But other influences, both internal and external to the child, affect his development, particularly influences of a cultural nature such as myths and legends. Fairy stories, trees, hills, clouds, running water, flowers, insects are all liable to be incorporated into a child's fantasies and linked up with masturbation.

It may well be that at an important time in his early sexual development the child comes into physical contact with some object that either acts as a stimulus to masturbation or potentiates his pleasurable sensations. Stimulus, masturbatory pleasure and fantasies become linked increasingly strongly with repetition. Rubber and plastic sheets are encountered by most young children, and rubber and plastic fetishists are common. The more the child masturbates to his fantasy in the presence of the by now pleasurable object, or simply with it in his fantasy, the more he reinforces and strengthens the association. Guilt fails to diminish the nature and strength of either the fantasy or the deviation, because sexual pleasure comes first.

Around puberty adolescents begin to have fantasies that have now almost reached their final outline. Understandably, the adolescent with fantasies outside what he considers to be socially acceptable may fear, perhaps with some justification, that he will never be able to lead a normal sex life. Despair and anxiety may then cause him to withdraw into himself and rely more and more on fantasy and masturbation.

Our understanding of the formation and effects of fantasies and fetishes, along with many other aspects of our sexuality, is still abysmally poor. Fantasies in particular remain shrouded in the mysteries, taboos and fears of childhood. It is tragic for mankind that so many people are still unwilling to accept the concept of childhood sex and ultimately their own sexual fantasies.

4 Marriage and Sexual Fantasies

Love is an ideal thing, marriage a real thing; a confusion
of the real with the ideal never goes unpunished.

Goethe

The previous chapter described how sexual fantasies develop
out of the experiences of childhood and for the most part
are firmly formed by adolescence or early adulthood. For
most teenage boys and many teenage girls sexual fantasies
are gratified or acted out through masturbation. Masturbation is the means whereby their fears and fantasies are
modified and adapted to the needs of reality.

But masturbation is a solitary activity, usually invoking
sadistic or masochistic fantasies and likely, for a time at any
rate, to be superseded by love. As though by the wave of a
magic wand, the chosen person is suddenly transformed into
a superior being, and all his or her attributes are idealized:
the woman lovely, perfect, admirable and good; the man
brave, strong yet gentle, often the antithesis of sexual fantasy figures. 'How beautiful you are, my dearest, how
beautiful, your eyes are like doves!' whispers the lover.
Only those in love can recognize the transformation into the
phoenix lover risen from the incinerator flames. For a while
the lover is anxious and self-doubting. Yet, miraculously, it
seems that his love is accepted and returned. The lovers'
everyday lives are transformed by love. Colours are brighter,

people appear to be more attractive and friendly, work is interesting, there is an increased sense of purpose and joy in life and no obstacle seems insurmountable. Each still feels vaguely unworthy of the other's love, but their self-esteem is now high and they feel themselves to be superior to others.

Masturbation ceases or becomes infrequent. Those previously compelling sado-masochistic fantasies lose their power. The lover feels shame when he recalls them (or rather if they intrude into his thoughts). How shocked the loved one would be if she knew about them, he reflects. The gulf between masturbation and the beloved appears infinite, as far as heaven from hell. The sense of submission that one lover feels towards the other is based on a wish to please and adore. It is totally different from the humiliating submission of a masturbatory fantasy.

Love and Lust

Love is a state of mind and feeling, always involving some degree of idealization, liking, respect, companionship, shared interests, altruism, trust, possessiveness, fantasies and, usually but not invariably, sexual attraction (which is based on lust). Lovers long to possess and be possessed by one another. 'My beloved is mine and I am his', and 'My true love hath my heart and I have his', are characteristic lovers' sentiments, indicating a desire for total commitment. To be united for ever is the lovers' dearest wish, and death sometimes seems preferable to life without the loved one, as many pop songs and much romantic poetry demonstrate:

> 'The night is dreary,
> He cometh not,' she said;
> She said, 'I am aweary, aweary,
> I would that I were dead!'

And in *Wuthering Heights* Heathcliff says, after Cathy's death: 'I cannot live without my life! I cannot live without my soul.'

Occasionally it seems almost as though love and death are synonymous, that only when the beloved is dead can he or she be loved perfectly. Here of course we are moving away from love, back towards sexual fantasy hidden beneath a shroud of idealization. One is reminded of Edgar Allan Poe's necrophilia, of the sadism underlying much of his writing, and the way love so often merges with death:

But we loved with a love that was more than love . . . .
     [declared Annabel Lee's lover]
And so, all the night tide, I lie down by the side
Of my darling – my darling – my life, my bride,
In the sepulchre there by the sea, in her tomb by the sounding sea.

However, most lovers prefer to be alive, exploring and discovering each others' bodies and minds, and eventually making love together. But for this to happen and be satisfying, lust as well as love must exist.

Lust is a strong physical desire for another person. The *Oxford English Dictionary* defines it as 'sensuous appetite regarded as sinful', and 'lascivious passion' – exciting but socially frowned upon. The man or woman who is the object of undiluted lust is seen and described in terms that are often uncomplimentary: 'a greedy sexy bitch', 'a beautiful sadistic bastard', 'just a good-time girl without a soul'. No lover would dream of using such phrases about his beloved. Lust, in fact, is always associated with sexual fantasies.

Lustful encounters are useful, perhaps necessary for psychosexual development. They enable people to modify their fantasies and to become more confident about their sexual abilities. A purely lustful relationship, based on fantasies only, will not last long, rarely more than a year. Most short-lived marriages are based on lust and the breakdown is inevitable. Many of the refugees from such marriages rapidly marry again, usually choosing someone remarkably like their last partner, with similar results.

Nor will a relationship based entirely on love be any more satisfactory or enduring. A loving relationship in the absence of lust is as lopsided as one based wholly on lust and just as liable to founder, unless the sex drive of both partners is low and there are many shared non-sexual interests. Both lust and love are necessary for a satisfying, developing, lasting union between two people.

Sexual intercourse and masturbation do not differ radically, for both depend upon evoking similar fantasies. Each partner's fantasies, ideally, are aroused by and attached to the other. For a time reality and fantasy become one. When two people love one another they should feel free to release their sado-masochistic fantasies on one another, to enjoy them directly, rather than suppress or displace them into non-sexual activities. Alas! few do.

Premarital intercourse is taken for granted by many people today, although not always approvingly. The outcome of any discussion on the subject is all too often clouded by the participants' own sexual fantasies. Yet the majority of premarital copulators have a steady relationship with one person, which generally ends in marriage. Most engaged couples today expect a trial run before marriage, 'to make sure everything works properly'. Yet, in.spite of this, not a few marriages are dull and sexually unsatisfying, and break up or simply wither away.

Why should a man or woman be afraid to make love? For the majority who believe in contraception, the pill and other modern precautions have virtually banished the risk of pregnancy (although a number of women still don't take contraceptive precautions and 'inadvertently' become pregnant). Can it be that *he* is afraid of *her*, and if so, why? Her face and figure are divine. Her breath is sweet-smelling.

She is intelligent, artistic, a good talker, humorous, liked and admired by all his male friends. He finds her attractive and enjoys kissing her on the sofa. His penis erects, only to collapse when she hints at intercourse. Is it simply fear of failure? Yet he has performed adequately with a call girl in the past.

It is, of course, natural for a man to be nervous when he first attempts intercourse. He has doubts about his potency, about whether he can meet his partner's expectations, about how she will react to his lovemaking. But all these fears disappear with success. A woman, too, although longing to succumb to her lover's advances, may inexplicably feel detached and frigid just when she most wants to respond. But initially, for anatomical reasons, sexual difficulties are more likely to afflict a man than his partner. Only an erect penis will banish his doubts and fears and demonstrate to his partner his credibility as a lover.

Billy became engaged on his twenty-third birthday. He and his fiancée tried to make love several times, but he was always unable to obtain an erection. He was a virgin, but his sex drive was reasonably strong and he masturbated three or four times a week. His fantasies were of himself capturing and beating nubile young women. These, and the desire to masturbate, stopped soon after his engagement. Whenever he tried to think of them only his fiancée's face came to mind. And without fantasy he was sexually 'as dead as a duck'. The more he failed the more he idealized his fiancée. He searched for excuses: he was 'run down', overworked at the office, had mumps as a child, was hit there by a cricket ball . . . Only Billy's partner can reassure him at this point, gradually reduce his anxiety and so break the vicious circle.

She can attempt to explore and revive his sexual fantasies, even enter into them by encouraging Billy to act them out with her. But this is not without danger, for she may be so repelled by them that, although sincerely sympathizing with him, she is no longer attracted by his personality. But break out of the vicious circle he must, otherwise he is doomed to perpetual failure with her and anyone like her, and will be potent only with a woman he can regard as inferior, and therefore dominate and humiliate.

Impotence wrecks a man's self-confidence and begets anxiety. Failure breeds failure and soon the mere thought of attempting intercourse causes him to break out in a sweat of fear. An impotent man is no man in the eyes of a woman, no matter how much she likes or even loves him, and sooner or later she begins to grow resentful and to repel his by now increasingly half-hearted sexual overtures.

Masochistic men relapse easily into despair. Fantasies of 'castrating' women sometimes follow. Michael's wife left him after only two months' marriage, angry that he wouldn't make love to her ('I couldn't, not wouldn't,' the unfortunate man said). As Michael gradually became resigned to the loss of his wife his sexual appetite returned. He masturbated to a fantasy of African natives capturing and torturing a white explorer, the climax coinciding with the chieftain's wife about to bite off his genitals.

Sadistic men masturbate frantically during periods of impotence, seeking reassurance through their sexual fantasies, where they are all-powerful and in control. Both masochistic and sadistic men will sometimes go to prostitutes or ex-mistresses to convince themselves that they are still potent. But even when they do discover that they can make love adequately to other women, the real problem remains. They cannot make love to one particular woman.

Eric was a thirty-year-old bus driver, quiet and retiring, proud of his long accident-free work record. He and his wife became increasingly estranged after five years of marriage, and eventually she went to her doctor for help. 'I don't know what's wrong between us,' she explained, 'but he won't talk to me about anything except chess. And we haven't had sex for months. All he does is read books on chess when he's at home, and work out chess problems. He's driving me crazy.'

Eric reluctantly complied with the doctor's request to see him. After ten minutes or so he opened up about himself and volunteered that he saw himself as a chessboard across which pieces (i.e. people) moved. Sometimes he saw his wife as a chessboard. Eric dried up totally after this disclosure and sat looking uncomfortable. Instinctively the doctor asked, 'You mean you see yourself cutting her up into sixty-four squares like a chessboard?'

The effect of this rhetorical question on Eric was dramatic. He started to sweat and tremble, muttered incoherently and then burst into tears. 'That's why I can't touch her any more. I couldn't carve her up, I love her. So I play chess, think of chess, talk of chess all the time I'm with her, just so as not to think of it.'

After much hesitation he agreed to discuss all this with his wife, in the doctor's presence. His wife took it in her stride and said that she couldn't see why he was so upset about the matter. Next week they came back together, both smiling. Eric explained, 'I just drew the squares on her. It's funny, but it's made me feel a different person, as though I've just met my wife.'

Sometimes, of course, the apparent difficulty affects mainly the female partner. A woman with strongly sadistic or masochistic fantasies may be too nervous at first to allow penetration, but this is uncommon compared to impotence.

Joanne was still a virgin after a year of marriage. 'I'm so small and he looks so huge,' she explained. She had appealed to gynaecologists and surgeons to help her lose her virginity and 'make my long-suffering husband happy'. Dilators had been passed with ease, but the mere thought of her husband's erect penis made her pelvic muscles contract excessively. Joanne's fantasies were of an extremely sadistic nature, of men and women beating one another to the point of drawing blood. Only when this was discussed and related to her husband's masochistic fantasies did she become sufficiently relaxed to permit intercourse.

Most sexual difficulties arise because of a psychological incompatibility between the fantasies of a man (or a woman) and his regard for his partner: the man with strong sadistic fantasies cannot permit them to engulf the woman he idealizes; the woman's masochistic fantasies of rape and slavery fail to be kindled by her kind, considerate husband. Anxiety arises, and also helps to banish fantasies and desire, and a vicious circle is completed. When fantasies are blocked in this way a compulsive need to masturbate may develop, reinforcing still more the split between fantasy and partner.

A typical example is Anne and Kevin, a couple who got on splendidly while engaged. They had agreed not to have intercourse before marriage, he because of his High Church principles, she from fear of becoming pregnant. Before marriage she had no doubts about his potency. When they kissed and petted his penis became excitingly large. But the honeymoon was a disaster from the sexual point of view: Kevin couldn't maintain an erection for more than a few seconds and was unable to penetrate. After six months of increasing frustration Anne insisted that he do something about the problem. He refused. 'I know that sex is only a part of marriage, but I can't live with a man like this,' Anne declared, as she packed her bags and left.

Another couple had a satisfactory sex life together for a year before marriage, with intercourse about once a week. Soon after marriage the husband's sexual need for his wife began to diminish and it became increasingly difficult for him to respond to her. Yet he admitted that he still felt attracted and responsive to other women, and that he sought relief in masturbation.

In neither case was there anything physically wrong with the man. The failures arose from psychological causes. Both couples maintained that there was nothing amiss between them. Yet marriage had brought about a subtle change in their relationships. The woman was no longer simply an attractive, lively girl in the eyes of her fiancé. She had become his wife, the future mother of his children. After marriage, her role had been transformed in his eyes, just as his had changed in hers. Examples like this, of fantasies compatible with a lover or mistress suddenly becoming incompatible as a result of marriage, are not uncommon. It requires considerable patience and willingness on the part of both partners to rescue such a marriage from disaster.

Role Playing

It must be admitted that the average person isn't in the habit of wondering who he is and what his role is *vis-à-vis* his spouse, or indeed *vis-à-vis* anyone. And yet we all, consciously or unconsciously, alter the ways we talk, think and behave in accordance with how we see the person we are with. For instance, with our employer we want to be seen as an efficient employee, and vice versa. But what role does one assume with one's spouse or lover? Ideal male or female, all-forgiving angel, unpredictable demon, parent or child, companion, seducer, admirer, rival? Generally the answer is a confusion of many roles, but sometimes in an order that may need to be revised from time to time if the aim is a living and lasting relationship.

But not all incompatibilities between fantasies and partner are necessarily unconstructive, as the following example shows.

Carol's parents were divorced when she was six. At about this time she was enticed into a car by a stranger and undressed by him. She remembers this as 'an awful time because my mother would keep talking about it'. She was a rebellious adolescent and enjoyed playing one parent off against the other. She disliked her mother, 'a cold fish', and idealized her father, 'so intelligent and brave'. Between the ages of fourteen and eighteen she had several boyfriends who weren't lovers. During her first year at college she fell in love with a fellow student, a man of twenty-three. She started taking the pill and they tried unsuccessfully to have intercourse. She was fearful, withdrew from her lover and prevented penetration. This continued for several months. The man was bewildered and afraid to force the issue and eventually he lost interest in her. She next became involved with John, a clergyman of twenty-six. Like the first man, he was a virgin, wanted to marry her and was 'glad you've kept yourself pure for me'. Carol was physically aroused by him and able to respond to manual stimulation. But she 'froze up' as soon as he attempted intercourse and he desisted. 'It's better we wait until we're married anyway,' he reassured her.

Carol's fantasies were of being raped and kept a prisoner by a powerful, over-sexed man. Ever since she learned the facts of life at school she had believed that intercourse must be 'dreadfully painful'. But underneath this fear lay an even greater one, that if she and John did make love fully she would have 'to surrender to him' and marry him. After disclosing her anxieties and discussing the reasons for them, she abandoned John without a qualm ('he never understood') and encouraged a number of other men to become her lovers. One, a teacher, eventually did, and she is now happily married to this man.

Impotence and frigidity are liable to continue indefinitely unless both partners seek outside help. There are and always have been plenty of 'virgin marriages' in which intercourse has never taken place between husband and wife. Non-sexual marriages are sometimes remarkably secure, perhaps because among other reasons one partner satisfies *part* of the other's fantasies. Thus Carlyle was a heroic figure to his wife Jane, satisfying her masochistic need for a hero, strong enough in her eyes to ward off other contenders. On the other hand Effie abandoned the impotent Ruskin after six years of marriage, married Millais and had eight children by him.

A wife always, in a sense, takes over the role of mother to her husband, just as he is a substitute for her father. Sexual fantasies have their origin in childhood feelings and experiences, satisfactions and frustrations, struggles for power. Small wonder that marriage often reactivates childhood conflicts and behaviour. The man or woman still wrestling with childhood and adolescent problems, over-dependent on a parent, lacking a sure sense of identity, is likely to meet difficulties in marriage, most obviously with sex.

There are many ways by which people 'protect' themselves from the guilt and anxiety roused by their sexual fantasies. Some men split women into good and bad types. A 'good' woman can be worshipped like a good mother. Like the Virgin Mary, she is above sex and does not therefore pose a sexual threat. (That is, not until she becomes fed up with playing this role and begins to express dissatisfaction.) By contrast, 'bad' women receive and deserve no respect and are therefore well suited to be objects for masculine fantasies, masochistic or sadistic.

When a man marries a woman whom he has over-idealized, his desire and orgasmic pleasure are limited, even when sex is possible. He has to be pushed by his wife to make love, even occasionally. He performs mechanically, repeatedly asking his wife if she is enjoying herself, has she come yet and so on. Or he makes love in a perfunctory manner, finishes quickly and abruptly rolls over to sleep.

Masturbation and intercourse with a prostitute or mistress are infinitely more satisfying to such men because of the lust they evoke.

A comparable sequence of events may develop when a wife is unable to resort to fantasies while making love. She may pretend enjoyment, so as not to spoil her husband's pleasure, or acquiesce passively and think of tomorrow's shopping list. Sometimes she achieves a satisfactory compromise and gets her husband to masturbate her after his orgasm, or masturbates herself. Her fantasies weave around another man, an idealized hero if she is masochistic, a physically attractive but inferior (to her) man if she is sadistic. Many a milkman and window-cleaner has become involved with such a woman, both in reality and in fantasy.

These are extreme examples. Most married couples overcome the worst of their teething troubles and settle down to a reasonable sexual relationship for the next few years, exploring and discovering one another's pleasure points and releasing inhibitions. Some grow confident enough to describe their fantasies to each other, although this is not without risk. One partner may be so disturbed as to become impotent or frigid, although such a reaction is usually transitory. But when one partner is masochistic and the other sadistic, each may be enormously stimulated by what the other says and wants. Many people tell each other complicated variations of their fantasies before making love.

Mary likes to describe how she goes to bed with another married pair, seduces the man by guile, is subsequently pounced upon and sexually assaulted by his wife. Her husband, in turn, tells a story of a powerful wild boar, the possessor of sharp tusks and huge testicles, which is attacked, overcome after a titanic struggle and then eaten by two tigers. A relationship of this nature between partners with contrasting fantasies is satisfying sexually, particularly when the fantasies are acted out in some measure. But all too

often fantasies lie dormant in a marriage, undisclosed, un-
suspected. Inevitably lust for each other gradually dies in
both partners, and sex deteriorates. Husband and wife
become physically indifferent to one another. Marital tensions and difficulties tend to arise, often coinciding with one
partner's spiralling success at work, or with the arrival of
children. Husband's and wife's energies and fantasies are
diverted into non-sexual activities, and indifference is
accepted for the moment.

Christopher has masochistic fantasies. He comes from a
working-class background and has built up a thriving business. Four years ago he married Vanessa, who is in his words
'an aristocrat'. Before their marriage Christopher had had
several satisfying affairs. He loved his wife but felt that their
sexual life was 'dull and uninspiring'. One evening he drank
more than usual and began to abuse his wife for not appre-
ciating him, for despising him, for being high and mighty
and 'behaving like the bloody aristocrat you are'. Finally,
provoked beyond endurance, she lashed out with her fist
and broke his glasses. To her astonishment he fell on the
floor and urged her to kick him. Still angry, she kicked him
once, then thoroughly upset and ashamed by the scene,
escaped to bed. He pursued her, begged her forgiveness,
demanded that she should punish him and finally made love
to her. She was so astonished by the incident, yet too inhibited to ask her husband for an explanation, that she con-
sulted a psychiatrist. As a result of their discussions she
came to understand and accept both her own and her husband's needs. Now whenever Christopher wants to make
love he addresses her as 'My Lady'. She, in turn, summons
the 'underfootman'.

Grace lost all sexual feeling for her husband after the
birth of their first child. She had begun to feel disenchanted
with him even before pregnancy because of what she considered his 'over-concern with work'. She became fascinated

and preoccupied with her baby's genitals, continually fondled them and fantasized about taking them into her mouth. The thought produced intense excitement and guilt and compelled her to masturbate to relieve the tension. Only when she was able to disclose this fantasy to her husband after some months of psychiatric treatment, did she feel sexually drawn to him again. He reciprocated by telling her about his masochistic fantasies. At Grace's instigation they acted out the mother-and-child fantasies, he playing the part of the baby. Both derived enormous pleasure from this.

Extra-Marital Sex

Another, often inadvertent, way by which fantasies may be rekindled and lust restored to a marriage occurs when one of the partners becomes involved in an extra-marital affair. A wife who learns that her husband is going to bed with another woman experiences a mixture of feelings: rage, jealousy, envy, anxiety, depression, confusion. Sometimes her reaction is to try to surpass her rival in sexiness. Suddenly the guilty husband finds that he has two rapacious women on his hands. His wife badgers him continually for information about how her rival makes love and why sex with her is so attractive. She demands that her husband, who may be semi-impotent with both women by this time, should copulate repeatedly with her.

Some wives dissolve into tears, to discover with surprise that this 'turns on' their husbands. It is men with mild sadistic fantasies who respond so well to such titillation. Unfortunately, tears sooner or later give way to anger, and this invariably causes sadistic men to 'switch off'.

A cuckold who discovers that his wife is having an affair may threaten divorce if she doesn't desist. But on the other hand, and particularly if the lover has social prestige, he may encourage her to continue on condition that she gives him detailed descriptions of what she and her lover do. He is sexually aroused by this, and by his wife's transformation in his eyes into a 'bad woman'. She now excites his fantasies in a way that was previously impossible, with the result that the marital relationship may ultimately be enhanced.

Luke's wife had a short-lived affair that brought many problems and conflicts to the surface. Luke is thirty-seven, an accountant, a regular church-goer. He is obsessional in his habits, dislikes rows and has difficulty in delegating responsibility; he has virtually no close friends. Eight years ago he married Lois, an attractive, outgoing woman. A year ago he discovered that she was having an affair with a neighbour, a married man whom Luke had always liked.

Luke's world was suddenly shattered. Previously he had idealized his wife: 'She was perfect in my eyes, beautiful and pure.' Now he saw her as shameless and deceitful. Whereas before he had enjoyed looking at her naked body, now he averted his eyes in disgust. He was obsessed by an image of his wife pursued by the neighbour, naked except for a golf cap, and having violent intercourse with him.

Luke's fantasies are sadistic: his usual one is of soldiers pursuing and assaulting a naked woman. He had never come to terms with this fantasy and masturbation during his teens had always been followed by guilt and remorse. By idealizing his wife he had been able to separate her clearly from these fantasies. Lois's fantasies are masochistic. At first she had been attracted to Luke by his strong personality and 'the way he took control of me'. She even nicknamed him 'God' in the first years of marriage. But before long she began to resent the fact that he worked long hours and spent little time with her. She resented even more his refusal to argue with her and his habit of treating all her complaints as unreasonable. It was in this emotional setting that she became involved with her neighbour. 'He was so kind and considerate . . . but it was wrong of him to make love to me.'

Although Luke soon recognized that he was partly to blame for what had happened, he was quite unable to alter his feelings of hurt pride. The neighbour had overcome and supplanted him. He was no longer God in his wife's eyes.

Luke's sadistic fantasies were now openly vented on Lois. He cursed her and accused her of being a whore. He made her tell him repeatedly every detail of her unfaithfulness. He saw it all vividly in his mind as though he were a voyeur. He copulated compulsively with her, but always in the dark. In daylight he was impotent, unable to rid his mind of 'that damned castrating man'.

Lois at first found the change in her husband pleasurable, and was gratified that he now spent more time at home with her. But eventually, after two years of unvarying criticism and abuse, she began to weary. It was almost, she remarked, as though he didn't want anything to change, as though he enjoyed the situation. In a sense she was right. He couldn't forgive her because this would immediately bring to an end the gratification of his sadistic fantasy. He would have to cease being a voyeur. He could no longer justifiably continue to castigate her. He would have to abandon once and for all his god-like role. And she would also have to cease subconsciously aiding and abetting him. Their relationship was slowly improving until recently. Now he delights in – and she feels guilt over – the psychological collapse of the neighbour. 'I always told you he was weak and ineffectual,' Luke says. 'You shouldn't have been unfaithful to me.'

Jeremy can make love satisfactorily to his wife only by thinking of 'absurd problems', like why an elephant doesn't have wings instead of legs, or why hippos don't have long necks like giraffes. Awareness of his wife during intercourse results in immediate impotence. His wife complains that 'he sometimes takes ages to get an erection'. He has tried to persuade her to help him by talking about large mammals, but she ridicules the idea. Jeremy's fantasies are sadistic and he keeps them under control, away from his wife, by such compulsive imagery. It is unfortunate that his wife is unable to respond because a rift is inevitable between them. Jeremy is already having an affair with a young woman with whom he plays at 'bears and tigers' with much sexual enjoyment.

There are of course many reasons for extra-marital affairs: morale boosting, boredom, scoring points off a partner, curiosity, vanity and even the inability to say 'no'. Not everyone is psychologically capable of having an extra-marital affair. Nor is every marriage capable of withstanding the strain, let alone benefiting by the experience. The betrayed wife or husband is often incapable of seeing the affair in perspective. At first he or she is too angry and humiliated to attempt to understand it and what it may symbolize. The initial reaction is usually one of outrage. Threats and scenes cover up feelings of inadequacy and sexual humiliation. Only when these diminish can one spouse begin to see the other as a person, to appreciate each other's needs, and understand what went wrong in the past. Only then is it possible for fantasies to play a constructive part in the marriage.

A wife's reaction to the uncovering of her affair depends on several matters: how resentful or guilty she feels towards her husband, how much better or worse sex is with her lover, how much she needs the security, emotional and material, of her marriage; social pressures and the presence of children; and lastly, but one of the most important factors from the point of view of the future of the marriage, the behaviour and attitude of the husband.

Many masochistic men find their wives' close friends irresistibly attractive. The motives behind affairs of this nature are complex: to prove to their wives how attractive and potent they still are, sometimes simply as an act of rebellion against a wife or mother figure. Less often women become involved with close friends of their husbands; and they tend to be much more discreet. It is commonplace, however, for two couples who are very friendly, who perhaps spend their holidays together, to become sexually involved with one another in what amounts to husband or wife swapping. Swapping is often difficult to control. One of the four may be less or more enthusiastic than the others. And jealousy readily flares up if one of the couples becomes too emotionally involved. It is easier to avoid disaster when larger groups are involved.

Gwen and Jackie have been close friends from their teens. They married within a short time of one another and, with their husbands, continued the friendship. Each husband flirted openly with the other's wife, but no serious trouble arose until after Gwen had had her first child.

After much protesting Gwen was persuaded by her husband to come on holiday as usual, leaving her three-month-old baby with her mother. But she fretted about the child's care, was short-tempered with her husband and could not relax and enjoy herself. One evening she went for a walk with Jackie's husband and confided in him. He sympathized and accepted her resentments and doubts as natural. It was as though he had lifted a huge weight from her shoulders. She suddenly felt very attracted, and impulsively hugged and kissed him. He responded enthusiastically and they made love 'as if we'd always been lovers'.

When they returned to their hotel the two others at once noticed the change in Gwen. Unabashed, she explained what had happened. Amazement, anger, jealousy, laughter, tears resulted, and the evening ended with Gwen and Jackie sleeping with each other's husbands. This continued for the remainder of the holiday, with apparently mutual satisfaction.

On the last day Gwen began again to think and talk about the baby, and suddenly wanted her husband back. Jackie said that she liked the idea of sleeping with two men ('You started it all anyway'), and suggested that the arrangement should be continued at home. A dramatic scene followed during which Gwen accused Jackie of trying to break up her marriage. She got her husband back but the friendship between the two women was irretrievably broken.

Group orgies or swinging parties are a popular and useful way of restoring vitality to some marriages. Ideally most of the people taking part should be strangers to one another. Inhibitions are then more likely to be cast aside and fantasies acted out. Fantasies are readily aroused by casual meetings with strangers – witness the ease and speed of sexual adventures on holiday. There are no deep and lasting ties or commitments with a stranger, since he or she hardly exists as a 'real' person. Lust holds the field, uncomplicated by any feelings of love. The presence of a spouse at the orgy, lending approval to his or her partner's behaviour, is reassuring and also creates a sense of sharing the experience. No longer can either view the other as an extension of a prohibiting parent-figure. As each sees the other pursuing and pursued, both their fantasies are stimulated and directed on one another, strengthening the marital bond.

Many people, particularly those with extreme fantasies, find the idea of group sex repellent. They are able to accept their fantasies while masturbating alone, or within the protection of a loving relationship. But the idea of intercourse with a stranger, of lust untempered by love, thoroughly alarms them. They avoid such adventures at all costs.

Of course disapproval of group sex may be on moral or social grounds, although not a little of this sometimes stems from ungratified fantasies. There are also aesthetic reasons, as well as the general inhibition of most people to expose their naked bodies or be confronted by other people's. Civilization obviously requires its members to suppress fantasies that are antisocial and sadistic. But much human unhappiness, dissatisfaction and destructive behaviour derive from the way people suppress harmless fantasies, out of ignorance and a sense of shame. Relationships that do not have fantasies built into them are likely to remain static and sterile instead of evolving. Small wonder that so many marriages are boring and uninspiring, that sexual attraction between partners so often fades when the initial excitement of being in love is over.

Sexual fantasies are not the be all and end all of life, or a universal panacea, but the man or woman who cannot or will not face his or her own and accept the need for outward expression is only half a person. Unfortunately, few do come to terms with their fantasies. In consequence many marriages never get off the ground and remain unsatisfactory and unsatisfying.

5 Pornography and Sexual Fantasies

Then what is the question? . . .
Gertrude Stein

The aim of all pornography is to stimulate sexual fantasies. Since nothing provokes excitement and therefore aggression as much as sexual fantasies, it is hardly surprising that barely a day passes without some new controversy about pornography being aired in the press or on television.

A perennial problem is how to determine what is pornographic and what is not. For instance, how many people will find this poem sexually exciting?

> Well I never, did you ever
> See a monkey dressed in leather?
> Leather eyes, leather nose,
> Leather breeches to his toes.

Not many! Yet to Andrew, a leather fetishist, it represents everything worthwhile in his sex life. All his partners are 'monkeys dressed in leather'.

Nevertheless, pornographic writings do possess certain characteristics that distinguish them from other kinds of writing. Because they are all aimed at sexual arousal, they tend to be one-track, and even if the writing does escape from its narrow confines it is likely to be banal and dull. There is **a** lack of subtlety and imagination. (Though, in fact, imaginative and sensitive people respond most and relate their fantasies to what they read or see.) Descriptions of people and sexual activity are gross, insensitive and leave little hidden; they are also likely to be monotonous and repetitive. Sexual pleasure is magnified into a Mecca of infinite gratification that leads nowhere. Everything is unrealistic. Men and women are able to copulate for hours at a stretch, with barely a pause between one ecstatic orgasm and the next. The man's penis is often of vegetable rather than animal dimensions – a prize-winning marrow or root – and the woman's vagina is capable of everything from frying an egg to vacuum-cleaning the carpet. The women are usually insatiable and demanding, able to fire off orgasms at a dazzling rate. Even after several hours of orgasmic activity the men are able to drench their partners in tidal waves of semen. Nothing puts any of the copulators off their stroke. Nothing is said or done that isn't erotic, and it is this uniformity and ultimate drabness that separates pornography from literature.

But the most characteristic feature, the one that upsets the 'anti-porn' crusaders so much, is the way in which people are made to be sexual objects, dominant or submissive, never partners. Contrast pornographic encounters with the relationship of two people passionately in love. In *Wuthering Heights* Catherine declares: 'I am Heathcliff . . . if all else perished, and he remained, I should still continue to be; if all else remained, and he were annihilated, the universe would turn into a mighty stranger. I should not seem part of it.' In *My Secret Life*, the author describes Sophy: 'she was exquisitely made – and from the nape of her neck to the sole of her foot was as white as snow . . . Sophy shivered, quivered . . . Before the first week of our acquaintance was out, she gave way to her passions with me . . . I was sick of the sight of her directly our bodies unjoined.'

Hard and Soft Pornography

Much pornography contains sado-masochistic material, with one person ill-treating another. 'Soft fladge', a term that covers minor sadistic activities such as spanking, is particularly common in porn shops (and is now creeping into girlie magazines), all of which reflects its widespread popularity in western society.

Pornographic photographs and drawings show an absence of human warmth and emotional feelings. The faces of the men and women are invariably devoid of expression, however provocative the position and attitude of their bodies. There is no danger of the male viewer feeling emotionally drawn to such women. Sexual fantasies can be safely projected on to them. Male nudes, once few and far between except in homosexual magazines, are increasingly being shown in response to female emancipation. But on the whole, women do not find these magazines particularly exciting unless they can identify something in them with the man they love.

More compelling than mere words, more stimulating than pornographic photographs that eventually pall, is the comic strip, particularly the sado-masochistic variety. Doctors and nurses feature commonly in such strips, but unlike the heroic, loving, unselfish characters portrayed in hospital romance novels and TV programmes, these are usually rather nasty men and women: a wicked neurosurgeon transplants a pig's head on to the body of a cretin which then goes on a sexual spree: nymphomaniac nurses force themselves on to helpless patients or blackmail doctors into satisfying them. Add a girl's boarding school, a torture scene, ending with the victim being disembowelled, and you have a popular comic strip story, read avidly by people of all ages.

Nearly all pornography is written by men for hetero-sexual men. Even lesbian literature largely exists for male stimulation. Pornography can be divided into soft and hard varieties, although the dividing line is indistinct. The soft variety includes girlie publications that are sold openly. Photographs of naked women make up a large part of their contents. Some of these are depicted as schoolgirls; nearly all are young, with hair flowing down to their waist, some wear flimsy négligés, others shirts only, their bare bottoms and bosoms featuring prominently in the picture. Leather belts, black stockings and polythene pants are occasional sartorial accessories. Sometimes the women are wrapped round with rope or even large snakes; handcuffs, knives and guns are other popular decorations. In the last few years pubic hair, long considered unacceptable, has appeared in these 'soft' magazines. The sugar-candied, all-American beauties of *Playboy* invariably had their thighs crossed, blotting out the offending region. Today the magazines are full of pubic hair – women with legs wide apart, nothing left to the imagination. At the same time much space is given over in the correspondence columns to the 'aesthetics' of pubic hair, whether it should be shaved off entirely or whether it is nicer if cut into a heart or diamond shape.

The more sophisticated 'soft porn' magazines such as *Playboy* include jokes, some illustrated, that are an indirect way of satisfying sexual fantasies. These cover a wide range of demands and include the sexual needs of old men and women, bestiality and even necrophilia. Letters, questions and answers, sex advice and a few articles (often concerning non-sexual aggression, such as imperial wars in South Africa and the Sudan), together with advertisements ranging from sex appliances to computer dating, make up the rest of the contents. Most interests are covered: straightforward coitus, masturbation, oral and anal sex, flagellation, and rubber fetishisms. The correspondence column also caters to all the more common fantasies (together with several uncommon ones).

Penthouse, a 'soft porn' magazine that claims a monthly circulation of five hundred thousand in Britain alone, categorizes its letters under various subheadings, such as 'Rubber Delights', 'Pain and Punishment', and so on. Other magazines devote far more space to the correspondence columns, adding only suggestive drawings and one or two pretentiously written articles. Most of these letters give the impression of being written in the editorial offices, their style is so similar. However, some people do like to write down their sexual fantasies as a means of distancing themselves from them, and some of the letters may be genuine.

'Hard porn' cannot be bought openly in Britain, and collectors have to look under the counter or visit Denmark to satisfy their needs. In the United States, since a recent Supreme Court ruling, each community may formulate its own laws regarding pornography. There is now, inevitably, marked discordance between one state and another. In New York hard porn can be bought openly. New York's sado-masochistic image, to non-New Yorkers, is thereby intensified, in the same way as the British view Copenhagen or Amsterdam. 'Hard porn' is much more extreme, has a smaller circulation, and caters for a wider range of needs, including homosexual (gay) tastes, pederasts (juves), bondage enthusiasts (bonds), tying up and rape, hard fladge and zoophiles (bestiality).

Women tend to be repelled by hard pornography, particularly when it is strongly sado-masochistic. There are of course plenty of women with marked sadistic fantasies, although they are easily outnumbered by men. They are as capable of horrific actions as men, given the opportunity: Salome, Delilah, Messalina, the female warders of Buchenwald. However, most of the women one sees screaming frantically at wrestling matches and other sports involving powerful men are masochists who want their favourite hero to prove his power by destroying his opponent.

Pornography also has different effects on virgins and sexually experienced women. Virgins are less stimulated by pornography and derive more erotic pleasure from romantic novels. Among married women, those with a good sexual relationship are most likely to respond strongly. Women dissatisfied with their marriage, who may not be able to gratify their fantasies with their partner, are particularly liable to express disgust and hostility when shown sado-masochistic pornography.

Men and sexually satisfied women often respond enthusiastically at first to heterosexual pornography. Men can be particularly excited by scenes depicting oral sex. Women tend to be more aroused by seeing and reading about coitus. Both tend to be unmoved by homosexual scenes, and the majority are put off by very unpleasant sado-masochistic themes. From the advertisers' point of view, one of the most interesting findings by researchers is that many people are less aroused by pornographic explicitness than by innuendo and indirect descriptions, which allow them more freedom to manipulate their fantasies.

Single unattached people exposed to pornographic material masturbate more than usual over the following days. Lovers and married couples make love more frequently and try out new techniques. They talk and think about sex, have erotic dreams, and are more aware of advertisements that use disguised pornography. But all these effects fade and disappear within about a week of exposure unless further stimulation is given. Even so, most people respond progressively less to repeated pornography, and eventually become bored. In the past pornography was used mainly for individual stimulation, but increasingly it is now being employed

by couples as a way of enlivening and widening their sexual
lives.

All pornography exists to create sexual excitement, but
all sexually stimulating material is not necessarily pornographic or obscene. Many reputable books contain passages
that are titillating, although this may be apparent only
when such sections are taken out of their context and looked
at in isolation. Take Fanny Burney's diary, in which she
describes being chased by the deranged George III in the
park at Kew: 'What was my terror to hear myself pursued
. . . to hear the voice of the King himself loudly and hoarsely
calling after me . . . on I ran, too terrified to stop, in search
of some short passage, for the garden is full of labyrinths,
by which I might escape. The steps still pursued me . . . Then
indeed I stopped – in a state of fear amounting to agony.'

Compare this paragraph with one taken from a hard porn
book: 'The Duke seized her arm but she broke free and
rushed screaming into the labyrinth. She heard him pound-
ing in pursuit . . . Her breasts [she is naked, having lost all
her clothes in the struggle] were torn and dripping blood.
He could follow her trail easily . . . She could go no further.
Trembling with terror she turned to meet her fate . . .' Or
this, from Florence Barclay's romantic novel *The Rosary*
(1909): 'Stealthily the Prince drew nearer and, with a
spring, seized her and clasped her in his arms. "Now, now
you shall belong to me," he cried. "You are mine at last,
and you shall pay for the hours of pain you have made me
suffer", and he rained mad kisses on her trembling lips.'

The Romantic Novel

The romantic novel flourished in the eighteenth century,
gaining in popularity as literacy increased. For a large number of women, particularly those who were single or miser-

ably married, it must have given, as it still does, enormous emotional satisfaction, providing outlets and indirect gratification for their sexual fantasies.

It is significant that most successful romantic novelists of the Victorian and Edwardian eras were either single women or unhappily married. (Some, such as Elinor Glyn, were clearly portraying their unsatisfied needs and fantasies.) Rachel Anderson points out that their tales are usually dismissed by those with highbrow pretensions as being harmless wish fulfilments for ageing spinsters, or relatively harmless escapism for the ill-educated masses. ' "But at least it's not dirty, dear" . . .'

The purity and wholesomeness of writers such as Charlotte Yonge (there are no kisses in *The Heir of Redclyffe Hall*, published in 1853) gradually gave way to physical passion. Rhoda Broughton scattered kisses prolifically throughout her novels. In *Red as a Rose is She*, published in 1870, the heroine Esther kisses her nice young man: 'At the touch of her soft mouth, that has been to him hitherto, despite his nominal betrothal, a sealed book, his steadfast heart begins to pulse frantically fast; if a river of flame instead of blood were poured through his veins, they could not have throbbed with insaner heat.' (Imagine the effect of this on a frustrated young spinster of the last century, spending the evening alone in her bedroom.)

Ouida, a contemporary of Miss Broughton, was regarded as equally daring: 'If you love me, indeed, leave me; there is sin enough, shame enough, spare me more. If indeed you love me, be my good angel, – not my tempter! . . . For an instant temptation seized him, like a flame that wrapped him in its fire from head to foot . . .'

Passion increased with the appearance in 1907 of Elinor Glyn's *Three Weeks*: 'A madness of tender caressing seized her. She purred as a tiger might have done, while she undulated like a snake. She touched him with her finger, she kissed his throat, his wrists . . . Strange subtle kisses, unlike the kisses of women . . . "My darling one," the lady whispered in his ear, as she lay in his arms on the couch of roses, crushed deep and half buried in their velvet leaves. "This is our souls' wedding" . . .'

It was E.M.Hull, with *The Sheik*, published in 1919, who first drew a picture of the delights of being raped by a virile Arab in the desert. After the heroine has 'fought until the unequal struggle had left her exhausted and helpless in his arms, until her whole body was one agonized ache from the brutal hands that forced her to compliance, until her courageous spirit was crushed by the realization of her own powerlessness', she falls in love with the handsome sheik in the best masochistic fantasy tradition. For good measure the authoress throws in some more earthy sadism, and describes how the sheik proves his love and at the same time kills a rival: 'With a terrible smile always on his lips, he choked him slowly to death, till the dying man's body arched and writhed in his last agony, till blood burst from his nose and mouth, pouring over the hands that held him like a vice.'

There's not a great distance between this bestseller extract and a paragraph from the Marquis de Sade's *Justine*:

And the two of us hurled ourselves on Olympe: Whore! we cried, we are tired of you. We only brought you here to get rid of you . . . We are going to throw you into the heart of the volcano alive . . . We gagged her with a handkerchief . . . tied her hands with silk cord . . . When she was defenceless we diverted ourselves by watching her; tears escaped from her splendid eyes and came falling onto her lovely breasts. We undressed her, handled her, and tormented her everywhere . . . At last, after two hours of the most fearful inflictions, we threw her into the middle of the volcano . . .

What they do to the wretched Olympe is not all that worse than what is done to the drunken Tralala, a decrepit prostitute in *Last Exit to Brooklyn*, who is repeatedly raped and left lying on the back seat of a car with a broomstick stuffed into her vagina.

In general, men fail to be greatly stirred by romantic novels and are not sexually aroused by them. The day-dreams and fantasies of many women are satisfied by such stories, with their veiled undercurrent of sex. Women leading dull lives are given a heroine with whom they can identify and, in consequence, be swept out of themselves into an exciting world of passionate love. Men usually require something cruder, more obvious, on which to attach their fantasies. James Bond gives them this. The James Bond stories don't appeal to women nearly as much, for there really are no females with whom they may identify.

James Bond and Company

The twentieth century has seen many bestselling thrillers based on sado-masochistic fantasies, such as Ian Fleming's. These are certainly not pornographic in a legal sense, but they contain many characteristics of pornographic writings. James Bond is irresistible to women, yet never forms real relationships with any of them and regards them solely as objects for his gratification. Power is the central theme, never love. He is superhuman in his endurance, virility and speed of reaction and he overcomes all his adversaries, in the end gaining some beautiful girl. (It is the fact that he is superhuman and inevitably wins through that relieves his readers of any anxieties that stimulation of their own fantasies may cause.)

There is a great deal of sado-masochism in all the James Bond stories. Bond is a real glutton for punishment and his adventures are typical of masochistic fantasies. In *Casino Royale* he is powerless, held by two henchmen: ' "Come my dear friend. We are wasting time." Le Chiffre [the baddie] spoke in English with no accent. His voice was low and soft and unhurried. He showed no emotion. He might have been a doctor summoning the next patient from the waiting room, a hysterical patient who had been expostulating feebly with a nurse . . . Bond again felt puny and impotent . . .' Bond has his clothes cut off him with a knife and is tied to a cane chair, the bottom of which has been removed. 'He was utterly a prisoner, naked, defenceless . . .' He is tortured to reveal information, by means of a 'three foot long carpet-beater, in twisted cane', coyly described by Ian Fleming as a 'homely object'. He is rescued in the nick of time, as Le Chiffre is about to remove his testicles with a carving knife.

In *Doctor No* Bond, this time accompanied by a beautiful honey-blonde girl friend, is again a helpless captive. Dr No tells him: 'Of course it will hurt. I am interested in pain. I am also interested in finding out how much the human body can endure . . .' The girl's fate is to be strapped down naked on the beach for giant crabs to eat her. Bond, however, is to be the first entrant for Dr No's recently constructed obstacle race, an assault course against death. Armed only with a table knife and a cigarette lighter, he gets through electrified grills, climbs up a massive vertical steel shaft, crawls along a burning-hot metal tube, watched all the time by inscrutable Chinese eyes behind plate glass. He fights his way through a cage of tarantula spiders and finally has a battle with a giant squid that wraps its tentacles around his body.

Sapper, the creator of the bestselling Bulldog Drummond stories, made his heroes considerably more sadistic than Bond, though they too find themselves in the power of baddies. His heroes, who are rabidly chauvinistic, are convinced that they have a mission to punish all non-British foreigners of dubious morals. In a story entitled *Colette* the baddie is a man named MacTavert, a pimp and a drunkard.

The hero ties him to a bed and flogs him unconscious with a leather strap, only pausing to remark how unfortunate it is that the cat o'nine tails is not available.

Both Ian Fleming and Sapper are essentially romantic writers, and their heroes descend from the archetypal goodies who conquer evil. Because the pornography is disguised and because of the protection provided for readers by the superhuman qualities of Bulldog Drummond and Bond, these stories provide satisfying outlets for large numbers of people who would probably be made uncomfortable and anxious by hard porn. Many an adolescent boy masturbates today while reading a James Bond story.

'Goblin Market'

It is of course all too easy to pick out passages of prose and poetry that appear to be erotic. (It is well known that the response to pornographic stimulation is greater if the person is expecting it, rather than if it comes unexpectedly.) Take 'Goblin Market' (1862) by Christina Rossetti, who was considered in her time to be a fine religious poet. This is a fascinating story of two sisters, one strong and moral, one weak and sensual, and their battle against monstrous goblin men. But for those people with strong fantasies of oral sex it is particularly riveting. Laura, the weak one, buys the forbidden goblin fruit with a lock of her hair:

> She clipped a precious golden lock,
> She dropped a tear more rare than pearl
> Then sucked their fruit globes fair or red:
> Sweeter than honey from the rock,
> Stronger than man-rejoicing wine,
> Clearer than water flowed that juice:
> She never tasted such before,
> How should it cloy with length of use?

> She sucked and sucked and sucked the more
> Fruits which that unknown orchard bore;
> She sucked until her lips were sore.

Once someone has eaten the fruit, the goblins disappear and can never be seen or heard again by that person, who pines and sickens from desire for more. That the fruit has some sexual significance is suggested in the poem, and it is well recognized that goblins and other 'little people' often symbolize forbidden sexual impulses. Lizzie, the strong one, goes to bargain with the goblins for fruit for her sister. She refuses to eat any herself, and the goblins hurl themselves on to her, squeezing their fruit against her mouth and face. Eventually, bruised and battered and covered in goblin fruit she rushes back to Laura and cries:

> Did you miss me?
> Come and kiss me,
> Never mind my bruises,
> Hug me, kiss me, suck my juices
> Squeezed from goblin fruits for you,
> Goblin pulp and goblin dew.
> Eat me, drink me, love me;
> Laura make much of me.

And Laura,

> She kissed and kissed her with a hungry mouth.

Many men and women are erotically moved by such lines in 'Goblin Market'.

Erotic Art

All art is, in a sense, erotic, capable of absorbing and reflecting sexual fantasies of all descriptions. Artists must inevitably project some aspect of their sexual fantasies into their painting or other work. Freud himself believed that artists' abilities arose out of their failure to attain genital maturity, and that sublimation of their infantile sexuality was an important aspect of artistic drive. However, works of art clearly depend on much more than the influence of subli-mated sexual needs and fantasies on the artist, although these may well have some role to play. If the viewer is stirred at all, voyeurism probably plays some part in his appreciation. 'The essence of the voyeur's position is his removal from action. He watches and participates in fantasy. His satisfactions come to him not through doing but through seeing what is done (or what is to be done). The simplest and most obvious subject of the male voyeur's enthusiasm is the naked female.'

The majority of onlookers obtain pleasure and relaxation from looking at an erotic work of art. As Edward Lucie-Smith comments: 'When strong emotions of rage are aroused this seems often to be due to the fact that . . . the catharsis is imperfect and the eroticism of the work is seen as a real and personal threat.'

Public Opinion and Pornography

It should be clear by now that pornography is expressly designed to excite the reader or watcher. But this embraces such a huge range of things that no one definition is satis-factory. Nor does it prevent a fairly sharp polarization of attitudes today.

Public opinion is divided between those who believe pornography to be harmless or even beneficial in its social and individual effects, who oppose any interference with the freedom of the individual to gratify his private pleasures or censorship of artistic expression, and those who see porno-graphy as degrading, destroying love, threatening family life, debauching public standards of sexual morality and propriety, and perhaps encouraging violence, delinquency and acts of perversion.

Lord Longford considers pornography to be 'a manifest evil', which is increasing and ought to be diminished. He receives support from David Holbrook, who sees pornography as violent and sadistic, reducing man 'to a state lower than animals'. To use Alex Comfort's phrase, many such critics are inadvertently 'professional manufacturers of sexual anxiety'. They aim at what, in the long run, is virtually a return to the dark ages, a repressive sexual censorship, on the grounds that the moral salvation of most of us is at stake and we can't be trusted on our own.

On the other side of the fence sit the believers in the sweetness and light of human sex, who have fought, successfully at this point in time, for freedom to depict realistically human sexual needs and behaviour, to 'free pornography in a civilized society'.

Certainly in the theatre and cinema since the decline of censorship those lonely men in dark mackintoshes have been replaced by less secretive audiences, more likely to be in pairs than single. Would Samuel Pepys, the diarist, have gone alone or with his wife to *Oh, Calcutta!* or *Hair*? 'Thence to the theatre . . . and here, sitting behind in a dark place, a lady spit backward upon me by mistake, not seeing me . . .' In fact one suspects that Pepys would have gone alone, for his behaviour seems characteristic of the sexually repressed and guilty. Spying a pornographic book in his bookseller's one day, he struggled with his feelings: 'It is the most bawdy, lewd book that I ever saw, so that I was ashamed of reading it, and so away home.' But a week later his desire was stronger than his shame and he bought a copy, 'in plain binding, because I resolve, as soon as I have read it, to burn it'. Having read it in one go, he masturbates and then burns the book, concluding: 'A mighty lewd book, but yet not amiss for a sober man to read over to inform himself in the villainy of the world.'

Kenneth Tynan is a well-known advocate of sexual freedom in the arts. He has no doubts about the function of pornography: 'Porn has a simple and localized purpose, to induce an erection . . . it is writing exclusively intended to cause sexual pleasure . . . and deserves a few words of exculpation and thanksgiving.' And again: 'The aim of erotic art is erotic arousal.' The editor of a girlie magazine with a large circulation puts it more euphemistically: 'We're catering for simple enjoyment at the sight of beautiful women.'

Scientists and Pornography

So much for conflicting attitudes to pornography. But what about the views of scientists in this matter, since David Holbrook believes that, unlike the arts, science has managed to retain a belief in man's dignity and creativity?

Psychologists and sociologists have certainly turned their attentions to the effects of pornography in recent years. Rosen and Turner in their investigations take up 'a cultural relativist position' and define pornography as 'anything which a culture defines to be pornographic' – which is only a way of saying 'You've gone too far this time', and doesn't add much light to the scene. Indeed most investigators are coming round to the idea that a satisfactory definition is impossible, and that it is better to describe pornography in terms of certain characteristics common to all types of pornography.

Professor Eysenck suggests that all writings should be graded on their pornography content, along a scale of 0 to 100. He claims that anyone can easily measure, by means of his scale, the amount of pornography in any given passage of prose. But this would, in effect, be more a measure of what Eysenck thought was pornographic than a universally accepted standard. For instance, how many marks would he give to the poem quoted at the beginning of this chapter?

Certainly we are not helped much toward a definition of pornography by D.H.Lawrence's view of it as an 'attempt to insult sex, to do dirt on it'. Pornography reflects individual attitudes within a constantly changing social framework of opinion. Even the law cannot find a satisfactory definition. Is it harmful, beneficial, neither or both? Without a definition it is difficult to carry out research into the effects of pornography. Most individuals are influenced more by irrational factors than reason, more by the nature of their fantasies. The more suppressed these are, the more violent the reactions and attitudes to pornography.

What research into pornography and pornographic stimuli has been done? Remarkably little, and what exists has little value. Students and other groups of people have been studied at random. Women's reactions have been compared to men's, different types of sexually deviant criminals have been tested and police records have been scanned for signs of changing rates of sex crimes when social conditions alter. (It has been claimed that sex crimes dropped in Denmark when the pornography laws were liberalized, but the drop was more apparent than real and resulted from the sale of pornography, voyeurism and other offences becoming legal. In addition there is evidence that the public in Denmark are now less likely to complain about minor sex offences and the police are less likely to prosecute offenders.) There is probably almost as much disagreement among researchers over their results as there is in the general public about the effects of pornography.

Attempts to show that sex criminals respond less to pornography than other people are unconvincing. In fact the methods used by researchers into pornography are thoroughly unsatisfactory. To measure responses by changes in penis size, dilation of pupils or the number of times the subject copulates, masturbates or has erotic night or day dreams is, to say the least, to restrict the problem. We need to take a broader view of people and to consider how pornography affects his or her values and non-sexual behaviour, particularly concerning violence, as well as their sexual behaviour, how its effects interact with social conditions and forces. At the moment we know very little.

Effects of Pornography

It would obviously be difficult to claim that the huge open circulation of 'soft porn' magazines that has built up in Britain over the past twelve years or so has added greatly to the sum of human happiness. Lord Longford would undoubtedly say No, it hasn't, and recount the pathetic tale of the young man, married with three children, whose co-workers showed him blue movies of middle-aged men whipping young girls tied hand and foot. He became so excited by the idea of this that he finally 'picked up a girl of, he thought, thirteen – actually she was eleven – who had experience with several men including her father'. (This reads like a letter to a pornographic magazine and manages to include so many titillating non sequiturs that even Lord Longford must have wondered at the tale's authenticity.) Luckily, and here the echo of Charlotte Yonge comes to the rescue, 'he was saved by the love and understanding of a "wonderful" wife'.

But some couples have certainly benefited from pornography, at any rate for a time. Martha read a 'soft fladge' story in a girlie magazine (it is claimed by the owners and editors that the proportion of women readers is increasing) and was sufficiently aroused to describe it to her boyfriend, Arthur, that night and suggest that he should tie her hands and smack her bottom. This became an enjoyable prelude to intercourse during the next year. But during this period Martha's attitude to her lover began to change. She increasingly resented his procrastinations over the matter of their getting married and having children. One night Arthur beat her too hard. Martha lost her temper, freed her hands, seized the cane and laid into Arthur, expressing in her violence her anger and resentment more than sexual lust. Arthur's procrastinations disappeared the next day and the couple were married a few weeks later.

Pornography had an even more directly beneficial influence on Janet and Bill. After Janet's parents, in their late fifties, were killed in a car crash, Janet, aged twenty-four, was shocked to find a cupboard in their bedroom full of pornographic books and photographs. 'They seemed such a happy, normal couple,' she complained. She was unable to comprehend for many years, during which time she became increasingly, although silently, dissatisfied with her own marriage. One day she saw a film with a scene of a woman masturbating, which disturbed her very much. Lying in bed that night she suddenly recalled her parents' bedroom stocked with pornographic material. She felt both 'sexy and angry towards Bill' and confused. Eventually rage got the better of her and she began punching her husband in the back, weeping and crying out, 'You dirty beast.' Bill, woken from sleep, was nonplussed and unable to understand what was wrong. His wife became so violent and distraught that a doctor was called and she was admitted to a psychiatric hospital.

Janet had had upsetting fantasies and dreams of beating and kicking people since her teens. Bill, after hot denials at first, admitted to strong masochistic fantasies. The pair were encouraged to discuss their fantasies together, as well as other aspects of their relationship. Their sexual life gradually improved and they accumulated a collection of sado-masochistic writings.

For people like Janet and Bill, placed in a reasonably stable environment, pornography can help to relieve frustrations and repair failing sexual relationships. On the other hand to use this kind of case history as a plea for more and better pornography would be a great mistake.

Masochism is, in a way, the cornerstone of human progress, and masochists have a better sense of proportion and reality than sadists. But a considerable amount of pornography is highly sadistic (possibly because it is much easier for the masochist to gratify his fantasies in other ways than for the sadist). In fact, as Edward Lucie-Smith has remarked in relation to European art, 'The greatest blot on the long history of European civilization is its addiction to cruelty – a cruelty often sanctified and made respectable by the machinery of Church and State.'

Pornographic violence in books and comics and on cinema screens and television abounds today and may well have a bad effect on some people with sadistic fantasies. In many cases pornography acts as a safety-valve, but in others it may have hidden perils. Sadists need to keep a tighter rein on their sense of reality than masochists, and continued exposure to films of violence may indeed reduce their self-control and in time lead them to act out their sadistic fantasies.

We know remarkably little about the long-term effects of constantly seeing violence in the media. It is almost impossible at present to predict what effect erotic sadism will have on any one viewer. Until a great deal more research is done, we shall continue to remain in ignorance. At the moment the field of pornography is bedevilled with 'investigators' such as the Longford commission whose committed stance almost automatically precludes the possibility of any objective findings. Such investigators merely muddy the waters even further.

Nevertheless, history has many lessons to teach us about how different societies cope with their sexual fantasies, especially sadistic ones. In times of social unrest and up-heaval – conditions conducive to mass hysteria – porno-graphy may have a widespread antisocial influence. Pornographic anti-Semitic material was used with frighten-ing success in Nazi Germany for instance. Any prejudice or ideal can be associated with sexual fantasies and used for propaganda purposes.

Sadism seems (to date at least) to be an inherent part of any civilization. Within a society there always has to be a scapegoat, if not an outside enemy, then someone who for some reason or another is forced into that role and perse-cuted. The Christian Church, the State, any large organiza-tion inevitably attracts people with strong sadistic fantasies, which can then be expressed openly (in a so-called good cause). The Crusades, the Inquisition, the witch-hunts, anti-Semitism, colour prejudice, civil wars – the list of activities into which sadism can be thrust and employed is legion. The power of sadistic fantasies has been seen all too vividly in our own time. No progress has been made over these instincts.

No wonder people rage against sadistic pornography, terri-fied for civilization, of what they themselves might do under certain circumstances. For just as most of us, if penni-less and starving, would steal a loaf of bread within our reach, so would most of us be at the mercy of our lusts and fantasies if the familiar framework of our society gave way. Rational thought is relatively weak compared to the power of instinctive forces. Social structures may change and our mental structures may apparently alter with them, but it is an illusion to suppose that the forces of our fantasies have diminished. We can never afford to ignore them, nor cease to wonder in what way they are influencing our behaviour. Our legends, myths and fairytales should stand as a continual reminder of their presence. There are forces in man oppos-ing his sadism. Perhaps masochism not only complements sadism, but also directly opposes it, and causes a collective sense of guilt to build up against prolonged sadistic excesses, so that eventually the tide begins to turn. Certainly this happened in the seventeenth century, after thousands of innocent people had been tortured and burned as witches.

6 Sexual Fantasies and Witch-hunting

In all the woes that curse our race
There is a woman in the case.
Gilbert and Sullivan

As civilization progresses, it is man's intellectual capacity that advances rather than control of his emotional impulses. Science and the arts together have helped to make us behave in a more humane and 'civilized' fashion to one another. But most of us are all too aware of how horrifyingly thin the veneer of civilization is. Over the centuries the violence so often brought about by our sexual fantasies has remained at a high level, interspersed with catastrophic eruptions from time to time.

Chapter 2 described some of the ways in which different people channel their aggressive and sexual urges into work and outside interests. Now let us see how societies cope collectively with their fantasies.

The Middle Ages

By the early middle ages social forces were becoming favourable for the witch-hunting frenzy that was to erupt violently

in the fifteenth century. Christian tradition had long associated women with the devil, condemning them as the cause
of man's exclusion from the Garden of Eden and for continuing to tempt men from the paths of righteousness.
Chastity was the only sure way for a man to win eternal
bliss: 'If thou wilt be Christ's clean child, flee as Christ's
coward the company of foolish women, nor be familiar with
any manner of women.' And since the end of the world and
God's final judgement were thought to be near, any sensible
man with an eye to the future not unnaturally came to fear
and avoid women. There were plenty of divinely inspired
misogynous texts to justify such an attitude, not least St
Paul's epistles. But, of course, fear of women went back to
even earlier sources. *Ecclesiasticus* says:

Give not thyself to a woman,
So as to let her trample down thy manhood.

and again:

By the comeliness of a woman many have been ruined,
And this way passion flameth like fire.

or:

Better is the wickedness of a man than the goodness of a woman.

Hand in hand with this widespread misogyny went
asceticism and contempt for the physical and its desires.
Lust and woman almost became synonymous:

> The beastly lust, the furious appetite . . .
> of womankind that dreads for no shame,
> Setting at nought God nor man's blame.

Monasteries grew up and provided places of refuge and intellectual stimulation, and of course protection from women.
Roger de Caen, a French monk who died in 1095, probably
spoke for many of his *confrères* when he wrote: 'If her

bowels and flesh were cut open, you would see what filth is covered by her white skin. If a fine crimson cloth covered a pile of foul dung, would anyone be foolish enough to love the dung because of it? . . . There is no plague which monks should dread more than women: the soul's death.' The fourteenth-century mystic Richard Rolle advised: 'Flee wisely women and thy thoughts always from them keep.' If this should prove difficult: 'Dost thou not know that the fleshly fairness is a covering of filth and the dregs of corruption, and often the cause of damnation?'

More sophisticated anti-feminist satire and literature became increasingly common from the twelfth century onwards. Its influence spread downwards from the literate, particularly the clergy, to the illiterate.

Yet side by side with such extreme misogyny went the idealization of woman. Both attitudes offered men protection from temptation. Just as God and the devil existed together, so the wicked temptress became contrasted with the pure virginal woman, personified by the Virgin Mary herself. Chastity and virginity were elevated above marriage. The cult of the Virgin began to spread from about the seventh century, but did not become significant until about the eleventh and twelfth centuries, when misogamy (hatred of marriage) reached its height. Convents multiplied as fast as monasteries, although unlike the monks many nuns were probably pressed into making their vows; a forced vocation, if it ensured that a woman retained her purity, was not questioned, particularly as it provided an easy and respectable way of disposing of unmarried daughters. At the same time, nourished by the peace and prosperity of that period, and no doubt by boredom, the troubadour or courtly love tradition was springing up, reflecting the beginnings of a change in the social climate, if only among the knights and secular ruling classes. The woman who was the object of courtly love was seen as pure and perfect, unblemished and unattainable, the object of desire rather than passion, a constant source of inspiration and goodness. Clearly there is not a vast gap between the troubadour's ideal woman and the ecclesiastic's concept of the Virgin Mary. Through such idealization relating to their sexual fantasies men's fears can be transformed into beauty, truth and goodness. Alas, as the middle ages waned idealization was to suffer a decline.

Meanwhile unrest was spreading through western Christendom. Until the eleventh century there were no heretical sects in the West. Now heresies began to appear, carried along the trade routes from the Balkans. These proliferated in the flourishing populations of northern Italy and southern France, reaching a peak during the twelfth century. The authorities, both ecclesiastical and secular, were alarmed and reacted strongly in defence of orthodoxy. Heretics were forced to recant or were burned.

It is a common human response to attribute to strangers and nonconforming groups of people impulses that are consciously unacceptable, particularly those of a sexual and aggressive nature. It is not surprising therefore that the clergy at this time, preoccupied for so long with suppressing their sexual needs and fantasies, and probably bubbling over with sexual guilt, should have accused heretics of collaborating with devils, of becoming Satan worshippers, and indulging in all kinds of orgies and obscenities. Demons themselves are nothing more than projections of man's fears and unacceptable desires; to associate them with heretics, Jews, witches or any other undesirables, even women, was a natural and easy process.

Leading the attack on heresy was the Inquisition, which was founded for this purpose in 1230 and was under the control of the Dominican order of friars. (St Dominic was an outstanding administrator whose fantasies, no doubt well disguised even from himself, were almost certainly sadistic. The story of his plucking a sparrow alive is particularly indicative.) The hounds of the Lord – or *domini canes* as the Inquisitors came to call themselves – had great powers, including the judicial use of torture. (Torture was forbidden in England under common law, and as a result England escaped most of the violence and cruelty seen in the rest of Europe.) Torture was applied until the accused confessed what the Inquisitors wanted to hear. They dealt effectively with such heretics as the Albigenses, and towards the end of the middle ages began to turn their attention towards witchcraft. The Inquisitors were all chaste, misogynous men, and must inevitably have had greatly distorted ideas about sex. The confessions they obtained from the witches bear this out only too well. After the confession came the public *auto-da-fé* and the victim's screams as he, or more usually she, slowly roasted to death in the purifying flames.

Belief in witches, superstitions, the power of the 'evil eye', spells and sympathetic magic has no doubt existed for as long as man. The early Church frowned on such pagan beliefs. St Boniface, in the eighth century, for instance, declared that to believe in witches or werewolves was un-Christian. Later in the same century Charlemagne decreed the death penalty for anyone who, in newly converted Saxony, burnt supposed witches. During the following centuries the authorities declared that night-flying and metamorphosis were hallucinations, and that the idea of a witches' sabbath was absurd. In short they were at pains to deny the existence of witches.

By the end of the middle ages all this had changed:

Those err who say there is no such thing as witchcraft, but that it is purely imaginary . . . this is contrary to true faith, which teaches us that certain angels fell from heaven and are now devils, and we are bound to acknowledge that by their very nature they can do many wonderful things which we cannot. And those who try to induce others to perform such evil wonders are called witches . . . such persons are plainly heretics.

Witchcraft became an accepted fact and all Christendom was seen to be 'at the mercy of these horrifying creatures'. In December 1484, Pope Innocent VIII was persuaded to issue his 'Witch Bull', authorizing the Dominican Inquisitors Sprenger and Kramer to search out and destroy all witches.

It has . . . lately come to our ears . . . that many persons of both sexes . . . have abandoned themselves to devils, incubi and succubi, and by their incantations, spells, conjurations, and other accursed charms and crafts, enormities and horrid offences, have slain infants yet in the mother's womb, and also the offspring of cattle, have blasted the produce of the earth . . . afflict and torment men and women . . . with . . . pains and sore diseases . . . they hinder men from performing the sexual act and women from conceiving, whence husbands cannot know their wives nor wives receive their husbands . . .

This was a formidable document and gave the two Dominicans very wide powers. Within two years they had followed it up with their encyclopedia of demonology, the *Malleus Malificarum* or 'Witches Hammer', which has been described as one of the most wicked and obscene books ever written. Over the next two centuries thousands of witches, mostly women, were to be tortured and burned. The *Malleus Malificarum* expresses vividly man's sexual fantasies, and in the hands of the Inquisitors it became a bridge joining fantasy to reality, allowing men's sado-masochistic fantasies to run riot in a blood-bath for over two hundred years before reason reasserted control over the concept of demonology. But before this was possible there had to be immense suffering. The Inquisition is a salutary example of the harm that pornography can do when the social climate is right.

The Witch Craze

The long-lasting witch craze stemmed, in one sense, from centuries of celibacy and misogyny among churchmen and ecclesiastical authorities, from years of suppressed sexual need and guilt. For hundreds of years such men had, for the most part, succeeded in holding down their desires and in controlling or sublimating their sexual fantasies. But when heresies challenged the orthodox system of beliefs the social framework began to creak and wobble. Once the faithful were sent to punish and exterminate the heretics, men relaxed control over their fantasies and gratified them in the service of God. Suddenly, after centuries of fear of women and suppressed sexual desire, sado-masochistic fantasies burst out and joined with demonology, finding witchcraft a satisfying and socially acceptable subject of attention.

It is highly significant that most witches were women. 'Why is it that women are chiefly addicted to evil superstitions?' asks the *Malleus*. 'All witchcraft comes from carnal lust, which is in woman insatiable,' answer Sprenger and Kramer. 'For the sake of fulfilling their lusts they consort even with devils.'

People accused of witchcraft were interrogated and tortured by the Inquisitors. Not unnaturally, most of the terrified victims confessed to whatever was demanded of them. As a result the Inquisitors built up an extraordinary picture of the obscene activities of devils and witches, the basis of which undoubtedly came from their own fantasies, aided and abetted by those victims with strong masochistic fantasies who were mentally deranged. Witches flew or were transferred from one place to another by the devil's power. They rode abroad naked, covered by a specially prepared magic ointment, usually accompanied by a devil disguised as a 'familiar'. They attended sabbaths, where all the witches danced round, worshipping the devil and copulating with him. The devil might take the form of a goat, or a toad or a tall black man with a large hard penis – a common fantasy of sexually unsure men today is of their partner being raped by a tall man with a vast erect penis; such men can be potent only when describing their fantasies aloud as they copulate. If he was a goat, the witches queued up to peer under his tail and, if possible, kiss his anus. The devil appeared less often as a toad, and then expected to be kissed only on the mouth. There was feasting and human flesh, particularly that of unbaptized infants, was sometimes consumed. Copulation with the devil was always painful, and both his embraces and his semen were icy cold. None the less the witches were thought to enjoy these carnal pleasures, which also bestowed special powers on them.

Although witches were believed to have the power, among other things, to spoil harvests, upset and kill cattle and cause wet summers, their main threat was to people's sexual behaviour. Through their evil spells they made men impotent and sterile, women frigid and infertile; took away sexual desire; turned one spouse against another; caused miscarriages and abortions. Many of the accusations came from disgruntled men who were sexually inadequate and general failures.

Once the Inquisition got under way 'witches' were discovered in astounding numbers. 'The devil was everywhere and the earth was his empire.' Witches were recognizable from the presence of blemishes and marks on their body; patches of hair, supernumerary nipples, warts, moles, birthmarks and anything allegedly looking like the love bite of the devil. Areas of anaesthesia were sought during examination and an absolutely diagnostic sign was failure to bleed when pricked. (The anxiety provoked by such an examination is quite likely to cause blood vessels in the vicinity of the pinprick to contract and fail to bleed.)

The majority of victims were women, although no one was safe at the height of the persecution. Many of them were mentally ill, suffering from schizophrenia, melancholia or simply senility. In England, where torture was not allowed, methods such as ducking and preventing the victim from sleeping for several days at a time were employed. On the Continent those who refused to confess were tortured horribly, racked and screwed, their nails were torn out, needles were inserted, limbs were crushed, until they admitted their guilt.

Men's fear of women is reflected in the fate meted out to witches. After confession, broken in body and spirit, the witch was led backwards into the court so as not to bewitch the judge with her evil eye. She was stripped naked, the marks of the devil and torture were exposed; her head and pubic hair were shaved so that no devil could conceal himself about her body. She was humiliated to the end, just as if she were a participant in the grossest kind of sado-masochistic fantasy.

England was much less extreme in witch-hunting than the Continent and far fewer people perished. None the less in Essex alone at least 100 witches were hanged (English witches were not burnt) between 1560 and 1660. The last execution of a witch in England was in 1685 and the last known trial in 1717. Finally in 1736 the Witchcraft Act of 1604 (brought in by James I, at one time a staunch believer in demonology) was repealed, although not without some protest.

Americans were much less affected. Although emigrants from Europe brought with them beliefs about witchcraft and witchcraft was a capital offence, there were few executions before the Salem witch-hunts in 1692. In this New England village, where there was at the time considerable social unrest and bitterness, hysteria suddenly broke out among adolescent girls, who began denouncing people as witches. For a year the villagers were dominated and put in fear of their lives by the fantasies of these girls, so much so that the whole community was for a time endangered.

During this period over 150 people were accused; nineteen of these were executed; one man was put to death for refusing to plead; and several women died in prison. Then reason asserted itself as sadistic fantasies became satiated, the accusers were recognized as neurotic young women, rather than divine mouthpieces, and the trials came to an end.

Witch-hunting began to decline slowly from about the middle of the seventeenth century. That it had lasted for so long was due perhaps to the struggle associated with the Reformation and Counter-Reformation, in which the protagonists of the rival churches accused their rivals of witchcraft and heresy. At times of social unrest and radical change, people seem to need a scapegoat on to whom they can project their fears and anger. Demons, heretics and witches were naturally linked together, certainly by the clergy who led the witch-hunts.

The laity were always more sceptical than the clergy, perhaps because they were less likely to be sexually frustrated and blinded by their fantasies. Many were increasingly upset by the cruelties, doubted the confessions obtained under torture and the ways by which witches were identified, and recognized that many 'witches' were in fact mentally ill.

The natural reaction of people with masochistic fantasies is to be sickened and angered by cruelty and suffering, and to protest unless it is dangerous to do so. Just as it was dangerous for a German to protest openly about the illtreatment of Jews in Nazi Germany, so it was for people to side with witches during the witch-hunting era. A man had to be both brave and rash to doubt openly the witches' confessions of satanic orgies and other horrid matters. He was liable to be accused and burnt himself at the height of the pogrom. But as the age of enlightenment dawned, as secular authority became more powerful, doubts were voiced increasingly loudly. Belief in the devil and his agents faded and suddenly disappeared.

A new scapegoat had to be found, something on to which sexual fears and fantasies could be projected. It was discovered in masturbation.

7 Sexual Fantasy and Masturbation

He who is in love with himself has at least this
advantage – he won't encounter many rivals in his love.
Lichtenberg

Masturbation is, and probably always has been, a more or
less universal human activity, a natural and usually satisfying way for people to gratify their sexual fantasies. Virtually
all men, and the great majority of women, have masturbated at some time in their lives. Yet considering that it is
such a common and important human activity remarkably
little has been written on the subject and though it has
become fashionable to portray it on stage and film, masturbation has still to become an acceptable subject of conversation in most circles.

The derivation of the word 'masturbation' is in doubt.
The *Oxford English Dictionary* suggests either *mazdo*
(virile member) and *turba* (disturbance), or *manus* (hand)
with *staprave* (defile). The old word 'manustupration',
rarely used now, was derived from the latter. For our purposes masturbation refers to a solitary activity designed to
cause sexual excitement and self-gratification. Usually this
involves direct manual stimulation of the genitals. The penis
or clitoris becomes engorged and turgid, respiration quickens,
pupils dilate and the masturbator rubs his way towards

orgasm. Rhythmic squeezing of the thighs stimulates some women and a few men to orgasm. Masturbation can also occur through manipulation of virtually any area of the body that has become an 'erogenous zone'.

Almost any object may be used during the course of masturbation, either to produce friction in the genital or erogenous zone or as part of an elaborate ritual. Nuts, fruit, candles, carrots, onyx eggs, sticks, rods and bottles of all shapes and sizes may be inserted into the vagina or anus. Over-enthusiastic and highly embarrassed anal masturbators are regularly admitted to hospital for the removal of wine or beer bottles from the rectum. Vibrators are increasingly popular.

Stimulation of the urethra, the passage from the bladder to the outside, by means of the insertion of an extraordinary variety of objects is fairly common. Toy railway lines, objects made of wire from the kitchen, earrings, pebbles and on one occasion a 0·22 mm. bullet have been thought to be suitable objects for urethral stimulation by members of both sexes. Some of these become stuck and lost in the bladder, sooner or later causing infection there and eventually requiring operation. One genito-urinary surgeon has a large collection of hairpins recovered at operation. Rubber tubes are also sometimes passed into the stomach, rectum or bladder, through which hot and cold fluids pour in and out. Not unexpectedly, women who enjoy urethral stimulation also enjoy catheters being passed into their bladders. Men are less enthralled by the experience, although a few do seek it out.

Means of enhancing masturbatory pleasure are equally legion: pornographic material of all kinds, vibrators, massage, Turkish baths, ghost train rides, group sex, stimulation in and round the anus by a finger or thin object and even car washes. Enemas are popular activities: fortnightly high colonic irrigation gives enormous pleasure to one sixty-year-old woman and takes up much of her thoughts and conversation. An almost full bladder often enhances a woman's sexual excitement during masturbation and intercourse. Some people masturbate to the idea of the bladder swelling up like a balloon, squeezing the vagina flat and gradually filling the woman's body. The list of masturbatory methods is almost endless. Most of these activities are mechanical, not much different from scratching an itch or brushing one's teeth and no physical harm is likely to result unless the masturbator's enthusiasm and sense of size and proportion go awry.

Any situation creating anxiety may provoke masturbation: before or during an important exam (Aubrey tells us how G, The Duke of Buckingham, used to masturbate while being taught geometry), in the airport lavatory before take-off, immediately after the unexpected death of a child or a much-loved spouse.

Masturbation is often both compulsive and repetitive. Flying, heights, fast driving, gambling, a pitch-black night, the Big Dipper, all or any of these situations may provoke fear, followed by masturbation. But the desire to masturbate can also arise spontaneously, triggered off by something that in itself is non-sexual, unfrightening and apparently innocuous. A walk in hilly country, the sight and sound of a waterfall, of rushing water, raging seas, trees, a bed of purple heather, orchestras of bees and crickets, all may call up a desire to masturbate. Particular smells are intensely exciting for some people – petrol, tar, glue, coal, turpentine, oil paint. Paintings, sculpture, music, are all capable of arousing sexual excitement without being openly erotic. Classical music has a strong effect on many listeners. Deep feelings are released, but they are pure and idealistic if attached to another person. Some time later, as the 'idealistic' process weakens, they emerge strongly as lust. The desire for copulation or masturbation is then strong.

One woman can masturbate and make love satisfactorily only against a background of Beethoven's First Symphony. One man is invariably impotent if he attempts intercourse to the sound of Wagner or Berlioz. The sense of exaltation he derives from the music upsets copulation, although some hours after hearing a concert of such music his sexual drive and performance increase. A schizophrenic man masturbates repeatedly to the music of Stravinsky's *Firebird*.

Pop music is sometimes capable of inducing considerable sexual excitement, but its lyrics mostly follow the traditions of the romantic novel, confining themselves to idealized marriage, or to unrequited or rejected love and death. Love is idealized and more or less separated from lust.

Dancing frequently gives way to sexual abandonment. This is undisguised in certain native and religious ceremonies, and has been vividly described by several writers. Most dances have a sexual component, which may be obvious or disguised. To spend an enjoyable evening dancing, mainly with one partner, is as good a prelude to intercourse or masturbation as a pornographic film or an Amsterdam cabaret show. Some people *have* to have an experience of this nature before they can achieve orgasm.

The compulsive eater, the compulsive masturbator, seducer, gambler, nymphomaniac, they are all dominated by their appetites, but are they merely greedy? On the contrary, greed is probably not an inherent characteristic of human beings. It is the product of anxiety, of emotional distress, and eating or sexual activity can be used to control this distress. For example, some people use compulsive masturbation like a drug in order to induce a state of relaxation, lift depression and ease mental tension.

When an appetite becomes associated with other sources of tension almost anything may stimulate it. Rosemary, a woman of twenty-six, always eats compulsively after any disagreement with her fiancé, whenever sexual intercourse is unsatisfactory and whenever she takes stimulant drugs like 'purple hearts'. John, a student, masturbates compulsively for a week or two before an important exam, and when he goes home to visit his parents.

Men and women are more ashamed and secretive about masturbation than any other form of sexual pleasure. Freud disapproved strongly of masturbation and regarded it as 'a poor substitute for sexual intercourse'. Yet if we look at it from a mechanical point of view, there is little difference between masturbation and sexual intercourse. Friction to and from the penis in the vagina, and against the clitoris, is not much different from solitary rubbing of the genitals. But like coitus, masturbation is more than just a mechanical set of actions. It involves, often more plainly than any other kind of sexual behaviour, *fantasy thinking*. It is this aspect that gives the subject its psychological significance. It also accounts for much of the disapproval with which society has viewed masturbation in the past, and for the lack of literature on the subject.

Emotionally, with couples well suited to one another, sexual intercourse usually – not always – is an incomparably greater experience than masturbation. For whereas in masturbation all is fantasy, during sexual intercourse it is possible for fantasies to gain access to the outside 'real' world by being linked with the partner, often swamping and blotting him or her out for a time. Whether or not this happens depends on a variety of factors: how much each lover idealizes or debases the other in his mind's eye; the emotional state of each partner; how anxious or worried each is; and whether intercourse is preceded by adequate loveplay and arousal. When circumstances are propitious, pleasure and satisfaction from intercourse rise far above masturbation. Indeed sexual intercourse can be a creative act, resulting in a flow of new associations and ideas, not only in terms of partner relationship but in work and other apparently unrelated fields.

Arnold wrote a widely acclaimed novel in his late twenties. Over the next twelve years he wrote regularly, but without his early verve. He lived rather a monastic life during this period, seeing few people, working hard and masturbating reluctantly. His fantasies were of a sadistic nature – handcuffing, tying up and beating dark, buxom beauties. When he was forty he met and married a woman 'who I knew intuitively would understand my needs'. She did, and for the next four years he and his wife regularly acted out his fantasies. His creative energies flowed again and he finished two highly successful books during this time. Unfortunately, after the birth of their first child, his wife lost interest in 'kinky sex'. Since then Arnold has written nothing, suffers from insomnia and has fallen back on masturbation for sexual relief.

In this case the block in Arnold's creative writing was released by making love with his wife. The outlet she provided for his sexual fantasies allowed his creative energies to flow outward into his work. But the marital relationship was one-sided, for Arnold paid no regard to his wife's fantasies. As a result these were suppressed and his wife felt increasingly frustrated. Eventually she became sexually unresponsive, almost repelled by Arnold.

None the less, masturbation does possess certain advantages over intercourse. It can take place at any time and in any reasonably concealed place. It involves no emotional ties and responsibilities. There are no limits to the accompanying fantasies, it costs nothing, carries no risk of venereal disease and is always available. And as one of the characters in *The Boys in the Band* put it: 'I will say this for masturbation – you don't have to look your best.'

Rousseau, a habitual masturbator, saw it as preserving his physical, if not moral virginity. In his *Confessions* he wrote: 'This vice, which shame and timidity find so convenient, allows them to dispose, so to speak, of the whole female sex at their will and to make any beauty who tempts them to serve their pleasure without the need of first obtaining her consent.' John Ruskin shared this view. He confided to a female friend: 'Have I not told you often that I was another Rousseau?'

Masturbation does not always result in a climax. Masturbators of both sexes sometimes find orgasm too painful to endure. In such cases muscle tension becomes so acute immediately before and during orgasm that painful spasm of the muscles in the genital and anal areas results. These people are usually able to achieve non-painful orgasm during intercourse with a partner, although it is rarely satisfying. And it is always difficult for them to tolerate and accept their fantasies. Intercourse can therefore never be really satisfying. Other masturbators like to keep their kettles just below the boil, to prolong their pleasures by switching off before climax, then starting and restarting. They tend to be obsessional men and women possessed of a huge sense of guilt about masturbation. Their need to prolong the action is more often than not a desire to put off the feelings of despair and loneliness that succeed their orgasm for as long as possible, rather than any aesthetic appreciation of the experience. Such people have struggled long and hard against masturbation and its fantasies. Occasionally they are successful to the extent that fantasy splits off from the physical act of masturbation: half the day is then spent in daydreaming, the other half in mechanically masturbating or 'bashing the bishop', as one teenager described his actions.

Compulsive, repetitive attempts to stop masturbating have a superstitious childlike quality: 'This will be the last time', 'I'll never do it again after next Friday', 'I won't masturbate again if Arsenal win the Cup', 'If I masturbate

I shall become covered in spots.' Some masturbators have a compulsion to wash their hands a set number of times after masturbating, often in multiples of three or seven. Others keep a diary and mark masturbation-free days, trying desperately to beat the continence record after each fresh lapse. Self-imposed threats are common among adolescents: 'I'll never pass my exam', 'It will spoil proper sex and marriage for me', 'It will make me impotent', 'It will make the tip go purple', 'It won't go down afterwards', 'I won't score any goals next Saturday.' Ridicule is sometimes employed: 'What a fool I must look to Grandpa' (dead, looking down from heaven), 'The Duke of Wellington never did it.'

Masturbation and coitus both lead to a number of separate but interrelated events: erection, orgasm and, in men, emission. Sexual desire (libido), like other biological needs, is made up of appetite and hunger. Hunger is a *physiological* need, inborn and unlearned. In the case of food, it is abolished by eating. In the case of sex it is abolished by orgasm. Satiety follows. Appetite is an attitude of mind, a *psychological* need, dependent on learning and conditioning. Hunger and appetite usually go together, each stimulating or inhibiting the other. Hunger may diminish and disappear altogether during starvation. Semi-starvation, on the other hand, more often than not results in tormenting hunger that dominates a person's thoughts and activities. Hunger stimulates fantasies, and starving men dream and think of food almost continuously. Often they plan the menu of what they will eventually eat down to the minutest detail, suffering agonies of indecision as they try to choose between sole stuffed with oysters or truffled partridge breasts. Indeed many starving people, after rescue and refeeding, continue to be obsessed with food and eat vast quantities throughout the day. Similarly people who for some reason are deprived of their partners often copulate frequently and obsessively after they are reunited. It seems as if the fantasies persist long after hunger has been assuaged, and in some cases are taken over and used by non-sexual appetites.

Without fantasy, sexual excitement is low: however some women maintain that they masturbate without a thought. Kinsey in fact claimed that one-third did so. But on close questioning (throwing embarrassment to the winds) it seems that most of these women do have fantasies, although they are often fleeting and vague; words like 'rock', 'funnel', 'string', and letters and numbers occur. One woman sees a differential calculus sign, others think of geometric figures and abstract patterns, and disconnected scenes of country and town life.

Unlike men, women sometimes have feelings during masturbation that are akin to religious or mystical experiences. Fantasies at such times are usually of naturalistic scenes, trees, flowers, mountains, rivers. They are long-lasting, sometimes continue for an hour or more, and arouse a sense of joy, of being at one with the objects in the fantasy. Mythical beings, gods and animals may intrude, but rarely other humans. Orgasm is sometimes but by no means invariably sought in the end. The overriding sense of unity is broken by desire. To achieve orgasm the fantasy has to change. The woman is then overpowered and possessed by a powerful being. For such women religious and sexual experiences seem to share a common source.

Some women, particularly those who never involve themselves emotionally with their lovers, may be able to have repeated orgasms in quick succession. This is regarded by some authorities on the subject as both desirable and a sign of female superiority, although the pleasures of such repeated orgasms seem to be small. Multiple orgasms like this do not result in much reduction of sexual tension since this stems more from appetite than from hunger. As a result, when sexual activity halts from sheer physical exhaustion, or even pain, a prolonged sense of depression sometimes ensues. Many women behave like this because they are depressed and are desperately seeking relief through sex. Nymphomanic behaviour is frequently followed sooner or later by depression and prolonged loss of sexual interest.

Many young girls go through periods of compulsive masturbation, usually when anxious and lonely. Occasionally such a girl will compulsively masturbate on and off through childhood into adolescence. After puberty, this behaviour may increase in frequency and become more open. Such girls are usually psychiatrically disturbed and excessively dependent on a parent.

Susan has masturbated for as long as she can recall. Around the age of nine she masturbated with the fantasy of being undressed and having her bottom smacked by one or other of her schoolfriends' fathers. Since puberty she has masturbated for several hours at a stretch, never reaching a satisfying orgasm, and feeling tense and uneasy throughout. Mavis, aged fifteen, masturbates with a photograph of her mother held between her thighs, and imagines fat, ugly men pushing her against a wall and taking turns to assault her.

Both these girls had lost their fathers in early childhood and their mothers had remarried within a year or so. They each hid their jealousy and hostility to their stepfathers by clinging to their mothers and refusing to 'grow up'. In each case the masturbatory fantasy proved to be a useful starting-point for breaking the pattern of neurotic behaviour. As these girls became more independent and self-confident they were able to move away from home, and masturbation stopped being a compulsive need.

Many women who cannot fantasize or relax sufficiently with their partners to reach a climax masturbate compulsively, often between waking and getting up. Elizabeth has been married for nearly twenty years to a stockbroker. She adores her husband and wants him to make love to her. But she has never had an orgasm with him, and has always had to simulate one. Several times a week, and particularly during the premenstrual period, she masturbates in the morning, lying on her face beside him in bed. Her fantasies are always concerned with mythical beasts and satyrs who pursue and overcome her sexually. 'If only Harold looked more like a satyr and wouldn't always ask me if I'd made it,' she commented. In her case masturbation was a useful protection against an extra-marital affair.

Older women, becoming depressed and anxious as their menopause nears, sometimes begin to masturbate compulsively. Sexual tension may have been rising for some time, and masturbation is sparked off by an erotic dream, or by reading or seeing something erotic. And what to one person may seem only a mild flirtation will cause the heavens – or hell, in the view of at least one woman – to open up.

April is in her early forties, a virgin, a capable nursing sister in a general hospital. After a Christmas party with plenty to drink one of the physicians started to make love to her, but suddenly thought better of it and beat a hasty retreat. Frustrated and angry she went to bed. For several months after this she masturbated frequently, visualizing the physician making love to another woman. More and more of her off-duty time was taken up with this fantasy, which became increasingly elaborate in its details. Her work began to suffer, she was tearful on the ward, and eventually she became so disturbed that she broke down. The physician, by his action, had caused a volcanic eruption of desires and feelings suppressed since childhood. She came to accept masturbation as a sexual outlet, *faute de mieux*. But she was not able to face the physician again and had to move to another hospital.

Compulsive masturbation, like promiscuity, has many causes, and is a symptom rather than a cause of mental disorder. A nineteen-year-old schizophrenic masturbates continuously when awake, fearful that if he stops trying to reach an 'apocalyptic orgasm' God and his angels will descend to earth in a second Armageddon. Another schizophrenic spends his days alternately masturbating and pushing strips of model railway track through the skin of his penis, in order to connect his 'two sides' and shortcircuit his thoughts of lustful women.

Although, statistically speaking, women masturbate less frequently than men, it is likely that the gap is narrowing, particularly now that we have virtually discarded the nineteenth-century view that it is wrong for women to have sexual pleasure.

Let us now examine how western societies reacted to masturbation and their collective sexual fantasies in the past.

The Rise of Masturbatory Myths

Masturbation is barely mentioned in ancient Greek and Roman literature. This is hardly surprising in view of the acceptance of so many sexual tastes in the ancient world. When the subject is referred to at all it is nearly always in disparaging terms. It would almost seem that masturbation in those times was an unfortunate diversion from military prowess. For instance Aristophanes' play *Peace*, produced in 424 BC, puts into the mouth of an old farmer the words: 'Now is the time to sing the song that Datis sang once when he masturbated in the midday sun.' Datis was probably a Persian general who lost an important battle. Eubulos, a fourth-century BC Athenian comic playwright, is quoted by later Greeks as parodying Homer by declaring of the Greeks besieging Troy: 'Not one of them saw a single courtesan, but they masturbated for ten years.' Needless to say there is no such suggestion in Homer.

Certainly masturbation does not feature in Plato's ideal world. And Hippocrates, the famous Greek physician, does not speak of masturbation, although he believed that the 'excessive loss of semen' likely to occur with 'newly weds and libidinous persons' might cause serious illness.

In ancient Rome the subject is also seldom mentioned, although the first-century AD poet Martial does make a reference to it that suggests that it was as widespread a practice then as now. For instance Book XIV, no. 203, attributes to one young woman 'such a sexy walk that she would make even Hippolytus masturbate' – Hippolytus was renowned for his sexual purity.

The Roman legionaries may have been warned against masturbation, for Polybius (c. 122 BC) wrote that punishment was inflicted upon young soldiers who abused their bodies. But the probability is that he was referring to homosexual practices rather than to masturbation.

St Paul is silent about masturbation, an interesting omission in view of the way he criticized sexual behaviour and praised celibacy. Nor does the subject of masturbation give the Early Christian Fathers serious worry, to judge by the absence of any written warnings from them. This may have been due to the absence of any direct mention of masturbation in either the Old or the New Testament. The Bible indeed fails to mention masturbation as such. But at some time during the eighteenth century the action of Onan, described in *Genesis* 38, which resulted in his death, was interpreted as masturbation:

Then Judah told Onan to sleep with his brother's wife, to do his duty as the husband's brother and raise up issue for his brother. But Onan knew that the issue would not be his, so whenever he slept with his brother's wife, he spilled his seed on the ground, so as not to raise up issue for his brother. What he did was wicked in the Lord's sight, and the Lord took his life.

Surely this is as good a description of *coitus interruptus* as one can hope to find. Onan was practising contraception, not masturbation. But there was no holding back this latter interpretation, which became generally accepted by the Church. Until comparatively recently the word Onanism was synonymous with masturbation, and described an act that was unacceptable to God.

Contraception, of course, had long been frowned upon in the Catholic Church, and was officially forbidden by the decretals, a collection of authoritative decrees begun under Pope Gregory IX in 1230 and continuing as official church law until 1915. These regarded anyone using contraception as guilty of killing his own children, a view that extends back at least to Roman times and includes masturbation. Martial, for instance, wrote:

Ponticus, because you never copulate, but use your left hand as a mistress, which is a servant of Venus, do you think that is nothing? It is a wrong-doing, believe me, indeed one so great that your own mind hardly grasps it, to be sure. Horatius copulated only once to beget triplets, Mars only once to make chaste Ilia give him twins. Both would have lost the lot if by self-rubbing they had entrusted their nuptial joys to the hand. You had better believe that plain Nature herself says to you: 'Ponticus, what you are losing by your finger is a human being.'

St Thomas Aquinas (1226–74) in the *Summa Theologica* insists that the only proper end to intercourse is the pro-creation of children. In his book he makes one of the earliest Christian references to masturbation when he lists four un-natural sexual activities, in order of seriousness: bestiality, sodomy, heterosexual perversions and lastly masturbation. Clearly the subject must have aroused interest during this period, but perhaps only in relation to its contraceptive uses. Thus the fifteenth-century Frenchman, Le Maistre, writes: 'Suppose the seed were not fit for generation, yet the evil of auto-eroticism remains.'

The principal textbook of mystical Judaism, the *Zohar*, which first appeared in the thirteenth century, was also

strongly opposed to masturbation. 'Masturbation,' it declared, was 'a sin more serious than all the sins of the *Torah*'
(the Jewish Bible). The views of the *Zohar*'s mystic authors
were generally accepted and as a result masturbation, meaning both self-abuse and 'wet dreams', came to be unequi-
vocably condemned in Talmudic literature. The initial
reason for condemning masturbation was again probably to
do with contraception, but objections on moral grounds no
doubt quickly followed and took precedence. Today the
guilt of many Jewish people over masturbation is, by and
large, greater than that of gentiles.

Medical Views on Masturbation

Theological and social interest in masturbation virtually
disappeared during the witch-hunting era. It revived as the
eighteenth century, the age of enlightenment and nationalism, approached.

As belief in witches declined other ways of openly expressing the social tensions that lay behind many of the accusations of witchcraft took their place. And perhaps in the rising
middle classes of the eighteenth century, fearful for their
newly won prestige, condemnation of masturbation struck a
respectable note. Disapproval of the practice had been
expressed increasingly by the middle classes towards the end
of the seventeenth century, and this disapproval snow-
balled as physicians and scholars directed their attentions to
the subject.

One of the first modern writers on this subject, Richard
Baxter (1615–91), the nonconformist divine and physician
famous for his understanding of melancholia, pointed out
that it was the fantasies associated with masturbation that
gave serious cause for concern. In his autobiography he set
out rules for preventing mental illness: 'Melancholy Phan-
tasms and Passion' should not be ascribed to God's spirit,

and he warned 'all young Persons to live modestly and keep at a sufficient distance from objects that tempt them to carnal lust . . . For . . . venerous crimes leave deep wounds in the Conscience and . . . those that were never guilty of Fornication, are oft cast into long and lamentable troubles by letting Satan once into their Phantasies . . . especially when they are guilty of voluntary active self-Pollution.' Baxter's experience with melancholic patients must have shown him that their self-accusations were always to do with the popular sins of the day. He lived through the seventeenth century, when the devil's power to cause mental and physical illness was being discredited. But irrespective of the fact that it was the so-called age of rationalism, men's sexual fears remained. How natural the switch from devil to masturbation must have been, and with what felicity the new scientists, the rationalists (children in their psychosexual knowledge), have given their blessings to the dogma that masturbation is both harmful physically and morally wrong.

Baxter's warnings were as nothing compared to those published anonymously in about 1715, in a book entitled *Onania, or the Heinous Sin of Self Pollution, and all its frightful consequences (in both sexes)*: 'This abominable sort of impurity is that unnatural practice by which persons of either sex may defile their own bodies, without the assistance of others, whilst yielding to filthy imaginations. It leads in men to gonorrhoeas . . . nightly and excessive seminal emission; weakness in the penis and a loss of erection. In women to Barrenness . . . and at length a total ineptitude to the act of generation.' Those whom it did not kill developed diseases ranging from epilepsy to consumption. Indeed the picture drawn of 'licentious masturbators' is terrifying: 'We shall find them with meagre jaws, pale looks, with feeble Hams, and legs without calves, their Generative faculties . . . destroyed . . . A jest to others and a torment to themselves.' Included in the book were letters written to the author from his patients, describing their miserable state: 'That damnable and accursed practice . . . that performance of Satan . . . my memory has entirely failed me . . . I am dull, sleepy and melancholy . . . my nerves are affected . . . my body is full of pimples . . .' The cure for these ills was 'Repentance, Conversion and Amendment', together with the use of the author's 'strengthening tincture' and 'prolifick powder'.

The author remains unknown, but from the way he writes he is unlikely to have been a medical man. It is easy for 'quacks' to take advantage of the deep-rooted fears of their fellow men. (This is one reason why the medical profession erects such barriers round itself.) 'Quackery' relating to masturbation is still seen today, particularly in Asiatic countries.

The first edition of *Onania* rapidly became a bestseller throughout Europe, being translated into several languages. By 1830 it had run into its fifteenth edition and it continued to sell widely and be reprinted for many years.

However the full impact of these views on medical practitioners came when Tissot (1728–97) rewrote the book under the title of *Onanism: or a treatise upon the disorder produced by masturbation*. This was first published in 1758 in Lausanne and was translated into English in 1781. Tissot, a Swiss, was physician to the Pope and as such had considerable prestige in the medical world. His views were influential in Europe and the United States, both on the public and on doctors. Doctors were becoming scientifically minded, although still God-fearing, and here were facts from a brilliant colleague, one moreover who was in touch with the Pope. Tissot therefore had the approval and the backing of both the devout and the scientific fraternity.

Tissot raised masturbation to the position of a colossal bogey. In a sense his *Onanism* is comparable to the *Malleus*

Malificarum, although its pornographic rating is low and he was unable to persuade the Pope to give it the stamp of approval in an anti-masturbation bull.

He claimed that sexual excesses of all kinds, but especially masturbation, were liable to cause widespread physical and mental disorders. In both sexes the worst effects were on the nervous system, for Tissot believed that sexual activity increased the flow of blood to the brain, and that the extra volume of blood distended and weakened nerves to such a degree that ultimately insanity developed.

Tissot's influence was great, particularly on doctors, who were mostly from the rising middle classes, and in turn on their patients. Voltaire accepted Tissot's views, although he observed that Tissot also quoted cases of illness brought on by sexual continence. He commented: 'What then ought we to do with the precious liquor which nature has made for the propagation of the species? Released incautiously it may kill you, retained it may also kill you.' Voltaire concluded that, so far as most people were concerned, masturbation and rash vows of continence were both a sacrilege against the creator.

New publications on the subject of masturbation and its ills multiplied and there were few prepared to contradict their dogmatic assertions. The great surgeon John Hunter, in a treatise on venereal disease (1786), attempted to speak out in the name of reason against the masturbation bogey. He declared that any harm resulting from masturbation came only from feelings of guilt and not from any physical effects. But his words fell on deaf ears. When his treatise was reprinted after his death the offending paragraphs were omitted and replaced by an editorial footnote explaining: 'Onanism is more hurtful than the author imagined.' However Hunter's commonsense views may have had some effect, for the belief that masturbation was a major cause of physical disease began to decline in the first decade or two of the nineteenth century. In fact it became impossible to maintain in the light of growing knowledge of anatomy and pathological processes. Only those diseases whose pathology and therefore cause remained unknown continued for a time to be attributed to masturbation: baldness, acne, some cancers, diseases of the eye. But as masturbation lost its physical terrors these were more than compensated for by the belief that it was a major cause of insanity. Doctors became obsessed with this notion, and through their writings and utterances helped to preserve the myth for more than another hundred years in the western world.

It is revealing to read the opinions of some of the leading psychiatrists and physicians of the nineteenth century, and to see how apparently intelligent men are for so long reluctant to break away from conventional attitudes and beliefs. Benjamin Rush, Professor of Medicine at Philadelphia, who wrote the first American textbook of psychiatry (1812), warned that masturbation commonly caused insanity. He went on to say: 'The morbid effects of intemperance in sexual intercourse with women are feeble and of a transient nature compared with the train of physical and moral evils which this solitary vice fixes upon the mind and the body.'

At the Salpêtrière hospital for nervous diseases in Paris Pinel, who did so much to abolish the chains with which madmen had traditionally been bound and to restore human dignity to mental-hospital patients, regarded masturbation as a cause of nymphomania. He wrote in 1809: 'Nymphomania is most frequently caused by lascivious reading . . . [and] by the habit of masturbation.'

Pinet's brilliant pupil, Esquirol, believed even more strongly in the evil influence of masturbation: 'Onanism is a grave symptom in mania; and unless this is stopped at once it is an insurmountable obstacle to cure.'

Open doubts about these contentions began to appear, chiefly in Germany and France, from about the middle of

the nineteenth century. John Hunter's views that the harmful effects of masturbation came largely from the masturbator's sense of shame were resurrected. Like those who had
protested against witch-hunting, the disbelievers at first had
to be careful of the way they expressed their views lest they
be labelled heretics and advocates of immorality. Flemming,
a German physician, writes typically: 'I hope I shall not be
accused of having written an apologia for self-abuse; my
object has simply been to question the correctness of the
views that self-abuse is so very often the only or the
principal cause of mental disorder.'

The open disgust felt by many Victorian physicians
towards masturbation and their out-and-out condemnation
of the practice parallel the attitude of some doctors and laymen towards drug addiction, abortion and other controver-
sial social problems today. Thus Dr Samuel Howe wrote in
1848: 'One would fain be spared the sickening task of dealing with this disgusting subject; but as he who would
exterminate the wild beasts that ravish his fields must not
fear to enter their dark and noisome dens, and drag them
out of their lair; so he who would rid humanity of a pest
must not shrink from dragging it out from its hiding places,
to perish in the light of day.'

David Skae, a Scottish physician, seems to have given in
1863 the first description of what came to be called 'masturbatory insanity', a condition that today we can recognize as
schizophrenia*. Skae's views did not make his more sceptical
colleagues on the Continent backpedal, but they did have an
influence at home and in the United States.

But as the twentieth century approached English-speaking
psychiatrists suddenly performed a *volte face* and abandoned
the idea of masturbatory insanity. There were a number of

* Schizophrenia, under the name *dementia praecox*, was not clearly
distinguished from other mental diseases until 1898, by Kraepelin. The
term itself was coined by E. Bleuler in 1911.

reasons for this. Mental illness was beginning to be better understood and a more scientific approach was being adopted. Syndromes (collections of symptoms) were being separated and delineated. Kraepelin, whose classification of mental diseases is still the backbone of modern psychiatry, was positive that masturbation itself never caused insanity, and his opinion virtually ended the matter.

Interest began to shift from madness (psychosis) to the neuroses. A great deal of fascinating work was being carried out at this time by continental psychiatrists – Charcot, Beard, Janet, Freud, the French school of hypnotists and others – whose work still awaits further exploration. Not unexpectedly, masturbation now came to be thought of as the cause of much neurotic disorder. Authorities like Charcot denied that masturbation played the smallest part in the development of neurasthenia. Others, including Freud and Krafft-Ebing, agreed with Maudsley. Their opinions gained the day, and during the late Victorian and Edwardian periods many doctors and laymen were convinced that masturbation could cause neurasthenia, homosexuality, impotence, frigidity, sterility and other sexual problems, even abortion. The similarity of the effects of masturbation to the alleged powers of witches in this respect is striking.

Even a 'sexologist' such as Havelock Ellis, who always maintained a fairly balanced view of the subject, when writing in 1933 was able to go only so far as to assert that *moderate* masturbation in people did not *necessarily* cause seriously pernicious results. He still believed that excessive masturbation, even in normal people, could cause skin, digestive and circulatory disorders, headache, neuralgia, and 'a general lowering of nervous tone'. And he thought that excessive masturbation, particularly when begun before puberty, was liable to diminish sexual interest and energy, and create sexual difficulties such as premature ejaculation and impotence. He considered that female masturbators ran the risk of becoming sexually frigid (a view disputed by Kinsey forty years later). Ellis also felt, although not so strongly as Krafft-Ebing, that masturbation might lead to homosexuality.

Freud's views on masturbation at the turn of the century were similar to those of his contemporaries. He thought that it was morally wrong, harmful and likely to cause neurasthenia. But as with so much of his thinking, he gradually revised these views and came to see that the causes of masturbation were of greater interest and importance than its effects. His attitude to masturbation by 1920 was probably an ambivalent one, reflecting not only detached scientific interest but also his personal conflicts and inhibitions over sex. For instance, when one of his teenage sons came to him for advice about masturbation Freud reacted strongly, and warned him off the practice in such a way as to cause something of an estrangement between them.

Ferenczi, a close colleague of Freud's, saw masturbation as harmful because of the absence of the preliminary love-play that should normally precede sexual intercourse. As a result tension was unable to build up to the levels necessary for a satisfying orgasm; it thus became partly dammed up and caused neurasthenia. Ferenczi went on to suggest that this imprisoned tension upset an inherent self-regulating mechanism – sexual desire leading to intercourse, to orgasm, to relaxation. Because orgasm and relaxation were incomplete, masturbation caused a vicious circle of unsatisfied desire and compulsive masturbation.

Many of Ferenczi's ideas were still fertile as recently as 1938. Thus a psychoanalyst wrote at this time: 'Legitimate orgasm in coitus lowers physical tension, this is not so in cases of masturbation, where feelings are pent up, there being no emotional outlet.' Wilhelm Reich took the opposite point of view, that masturbation was therapeutically beneficial and should be encouraged. His ideas are discussed later on.

Freud's views on masturbation changed in his lifetime along with many of his other ideas. At the beginning of the century he believed masturbation to be harmful in three ways. First, by 'excessive indulgence and inadequate gratification' it somehow caused physical damage. This set up what he called an 'actual neurosis', to distinguish it from neurotic disorders arising from the 'resistance of ego against this sexual activity'. Second, since masturbation permitted an important need to be gratified without any real personal effort or risk in the outside world (Freud was of course a puritan in outlook), this encouraged the development of neurotic, i.e. unadaptive, forms of behaviour. Third, masturbation in childhood might result in the child becoming 'fixated' in his infantile sexual aims, arrest his psychic development and so predispose him to neurotic illness later on.

Although Freud probably never completely abandoned the idea that masturbation had harmful effects, he increasingly came to look upon it as a symptom of underlying mental conflicts that were of much greater importance and interest to him. Although he eventually believed that it did not cause neurosis, he considered any adult who preferred masturbation to intercourse to be behaving neurotically.

An interesting discussion on masturbation took place among psychoanalysts in Vienna in 1912. Victor Tausk, a brilliant man who had a tortured, ambivalent relationship with Freud, and eventually killed himself in 1919, was the opening speaker. Some of his opinions reflect the social attitudes of that period towards sexual and family relationships.

Tausk concluded that masturbation damaged human society because of three destructive factors. (He referred only to male masturbation and either ignored or overlooked the habit in women.) These factors were as follows: by damaging a man's self-respect masturbation diminishes his capacity for competition; by perpetuating psychic infantilism it undermines the sovereign position of the man in public life and in his family; by damaging a man's potency it impoverishes his love life and enormous disappointments for women ensue. Tausk even suggested that male masturbation was an important factor in the unrest of women and their demands for emancipation.

The way in which Tausk (like Freud) exemplified nineteenth-century ideas on the harmful effects of masturbation and related them to the social problems of his day, particularly the feminist movement, gives an interesting picture of the early psychoanalysts. Tausk's opinions provide ready ammunition for those advocates of Women's Liberation who proclaim that psychoanalysis aims to preserve man's dominance over women.

Two of Freud's early followers, Reich and Stekel, who eventually broke with him, developed very different and original ideas on masturbation.

Wilhelm Reich was eventually expelled from the inner sanctum of psychoanalysis for his heretical views on sex. He came to believe that mental health depended on a person's capacity to experience orgasm fully or, as he put it, 'psychosomatically'. He extended this theory to include physical health and elaborated the idea that failure to experience a reasonable quota of orgasms could result in cancer. Reich's ideas attained and still have considerable popularity in the United States, perhaps because many Americans are so preoccupied with their sexual identification and the tyranny of the orgasm, to use Cyril Connolly's phrase. Yet Reich himself eventually recognized that although masturbation might be desirable, in the long run it was never fully satisfactory because the masturbator had no one to love but himself.

Welhelm Stekel regarded masturbation as a necessary and universal human activity. He concerned himself especially with the fantasies associated with masturbation and looked on masturbation as the only socially acceptable way of satisfying perverse fantasies. If masturbation was suppressed, he thought, sex perversions would inevitably be acted out and become more widespread. He cited such examples as a young man who masturbated with the fantasy of cutting off his father's head, ejaculating when blood spurted out. Stekel seems seriously to have believed that the young man in question was saved from becoming a parricide only by frequent masturbation.

Today we can look back smugly at nineteenth-century attitudes to sex and masturbation or to the witch-hunts of earlier centuries and see them as the products of fear and ignorance. But an age that has witnessed two barbaric world wars, the extermination of six million Jews and the purges of Stalinist Russia, and is still witnessing a host of minor wars, cannot afford to be too smug.

Up to now all human groups seem to have required a scapegoat from time to time, on to whom they can project their sexual fantasies, sometimes with appalling consequences. Only when we become more aware of our fantasies and their power to influence us, can we hope to avoid repeating the barbarities of the past.

8   The Dangers of Sexual Fantasies

The more things a man is ashamed of, the more respectable he is.

G.B.Shaw

We have seen that many people are ashamed of their fantasies and try to suppress them. The effects of such suppression can be unfortunate for the individual and sometimes disastrous for society – witness the witch-hunts of the sixteenth and seventeenth centuries, and, nearer our own time, the exploitation of sadistic and masochistic fantasies for political propaganda and to foster anti-Semitism. But is it always advisable to encourage the gratification of fantasy through masturbation, say, in contrast to within a good sexual relationship? Freud thought not, as we have seen. And there are reasons to suppose that he was not altogether wrong and that the censorious attitude of the Victorians to masturbation contained a germ of truth.

It is clearly unreasonable to advocate the acting out indiscriminately of every kind of fantasy. Many people would end up in serious trouble if they attempted to put their fantasies into practice. Killing, torturing and severely mauling one's lover are forbidden in most societies. Bluebeard, the monster of Charles Perrault's tale of 1697, who killed seven wives in succession, probably personifies a common male sadistic fantasy. From time to time this fantasy is translated into reality. Men such as Haigh and Christie, to name but two twentieth-century examples, compulsively killed their sexual partners. Gain there may have been, but the compelling urge came from fantasy.

Gilles de Rais, a marshal of France who fought beside Joan of Arc at Orléans, is sometimes identified as the original Bluebeard; but his beard was red and he had only one wife. He was tried and hung in 1440 for murdering one hundred and forty people (as well as for heresy), mostly boys whom he handled and fondled for his own pleasure while they were tortured to death. The story of this man's sexual aberration is as appalling today, five hundred years later, in its emotional impact as the Moors murders or any of the other recent discoveries of multiple acts of sadism and murder.

Sexual crimes always arouse public outrage, mostly for obvious reasons but partly because they stimulate people's fantasies. Angry protests and demands for punishment are a natural reaction to such events. Some people sail very close to the wind, but they require a partner willing to endure or inflict pain for pleasure or money. If they are lucky or sufficiently selective in their choice of lover they can project their fantasies on to him or her, and gratify them more or less directly by sight, feel, word and deed. Those not so fortunate, who cannot establish adequate outlets for their fantasies, must either struggle against them or resort to masturbation.

Some people – fortunately few in number – seem unable to control their fantasies or to find suitable outlets. Tension rises in them, causing the boundary between reality and fantasy to become increasingly blurred. Fantasies may then be acted out with disastrous consequences, as in the murders discussed in Chapter 2, which highlight the fears of people with extreme sadistic fantasies and explains why they feel the need to maintain a tight control over their impulses.

The issue for them is always how to recognize and separate fantasy from reality.

Sado-masochistic fantasies occasionally play an important part in the phenomenon of 'battered wives', and battered babies. But this is unusual. Most men with sadistic fantasies keep them strictly within their imagination. Some seek out compliant prostitutes. Those lucky or sensible enough to have married women with masochistic fantasies which complement their own are able to act them out satisfactorily at home. A man may 'beat up' his wife to their mutual satisfaction, but only within the confines of sexual enjoyment. Such a wife is not 'battered' in the forensic sense.

Sam is an engineer. He has been married for six years. His sexual fantasies centred at an early age around David's *Rape of the Sabine Women*. He is erotically aroused by the thought and sight of a well-covered woman suckling a baby. He imagines tearing the baby from her and hurling it aside, beating the mother into submission and then raping her.

His wife had no idea of her husband's fantasy. So far as she was concerned their sexual life was all right until a few months after the birth of her son. Sam returned home late after a party, having consumed a large quantity of alcohol. His wife told him to collect his supper from the kitchen because she wanted to feed the baby. He suddenly attacked her, beat her about the head and body, and knocked her to the ground. He then seized and threw the baby into a corner. She screamed and he began savagely kicking her. She was rescued by the neighbours who called in the police.

Sam is distraught. His wife is both angry and puzzled. She is reluctant to inspect her marriage in terms of sexual fantasies.

Naturally, when faced with the problem of defining

reality, most of us are liable to become confused. Beliefs, motivation, emotional states, tiredness, level of consciousness, drugs and alcohol are only a few of the factors influencing what a person thinks is real at any one time. Philosophers will probably continue to discuss the concept indefinitely. But for practical purposes most people are able to distinguish reality from fantasy, at least in the general sense.

The ability to make this distinction develops slowly through childhood. A small child half believes his fantasy that a man came down the chimney and broke his mother's best teapot which he just knocked over himself. But if he tells his mother this story at the age of ten or twelve he is probably either lying or 'abnormal' (that is, his mental development is retarded). Some people remain deficient in this quality and have difficulty throughout their lives, especially when anxious or depressed, in distinguishing between reality and their fantasies.

Ernest Hemingway was a writer plagued by his fantasies. Masochistic in nature, he reacted against his fantasies by playing the role of he-man. Whilst writing he felt he had to eschew sex in any form. He warned against making love during periods of composition; the best ideas, he thought, would be lost in bed. He tried to control his fantasies and direct them into his work, not always with complete success. When not working he required frequent sexual activity, direct and indirect, but he was never able to reconcile his masochistic sexual nature with his heroic ego, and in the end he shot himself, perhaps equating suicide with masturbation.

The suicide rate is increasing among young people, especially intelligent, artistic students, prone to existential and nihilistic ruminations, often psychosexually immature and fearful of their fantasies, and worried by a strong sense of inadequacy in their work and social life.

> But suicides have a special language.
> Like carpenters, they want to know which tools.
> They never ask why build.

There are of course many reasons for suicide and suicidal gestures, including the gratification of sexual fantasies. Gregory's fantasies concerned the capture of a young man and a woman who, after rendering him helpless, forced the muzzle of a gun into his mouth. This fantasy began when he was nine, after seeing and reading a comic strip story culminating in the suicide of a disgraced Prussian officer. Gregory had just gone up to university when, on his nineteenth birthday, he put the end of a shotgun into his mouth and blew out his brains. He left a long poem dealing with isolation, pain, and unattainable love.

For most of us sexual fantasies are easily recognizable as such. Even when we masturbate and allow our fantasies to take command of our thoughts, most of us can stop abruptly at will and return to reality. But for a small minority of men, fantasies under certain conditions take charge of the mind and dominate behaviour. The male transvestite who dresses as a woman can usually escape detection, or in any case will attract little attention and retribution. But this is not so with the exhibitionist or more serious sexual offender.

Indecent Exposure

Indecent exposure is the commonest sexual offence in the United Kingdom, with about three thousand convictions each year. The shock of being arrested and appearing in court, together with the inevitable publicity, is sufficiently great for many offenders to control their urges subsequently.

Gordon, a man of twenty-seven, was arrested a month after his marriage, having exposed himself from his parked car to a female petrol-pump attendant. He was traced by the police through his car registration number. He looked younger than his years. He was hard-working but afraid of responsibility, self-centred and easily upset. He disliked angry scenes and was quite unable to express his feelings of resentment openly. He had known his wife for most of his life, had been engaged to her for four years and had eventually married her only because of pressure from her. The exposure followed a disagreement with her, during which she called him 'a useless specimen of manhood', because he was impotent. He had masturbated since puberty with fantasies of beating and swearing at a fat woman until she cried for mercy. He exposed himself impulsively and recklessly, driven by the need to express his anger against his wife and to feel potent and sexually dominant. When first interviewed Gordon said sadly: 'She [his wife] is just like my mother.'

His wife blamed herself for the incident and was willing to co-operate in her husband's treatment. After discussing their fantasies, both separately and with one another, the couple were encouraged to act them out together. A year later they were having intercourse reasonably often and satisfactorily for both. The wife had decided not to have any children, as 'he needs all my attention'. Clearly both partners now satisfy strong needs in each other.

Another man has exposed himself at regular intervals since his teens. He emerges from hiding at the approach of a suitable woman and exhibits his erect penis. He usually chooses young women, who are likely to react positively, with fear or with astonished curiosity. After a satisfying reaction he runs off and masturbates. Indifference and particularly laughter upset him very much. When this happened recently he became so angry that he shouted and ran towards the woman. She in turn started to scream instead of to laugh, his anger evaporated and he hastily escaped.

The fantasies of most exhibitionists are of exposing themselves to a particular type of woman, followed usually by mildly sadistic events – remonstrating with, smacking or beating her. Masochistic fantasies of being whipped by the woman to whom he has exposed himself are unusual.

Other Sexual Offences

On the whole there is little risk of an exhibitionist raping or assaulting his victim – Havelock Ellis aptly described the action as 'psychic defloration'. Most exhibitionists are much too timid to progress to more serious sexual offences. But there is some evidence that men who whistle and shout at their victims or touch them do occasionally go on to commit rape.

More serious sexual perversions, homosexual and heterosexual, that may result in serious injury or murder are relatively uncommon today. Those that do happen are all essentially the result of acting out forbidden fantasies. However, sex murders in Britain are more often committed in fright than out of sadism. The assaulter panics when his victim screams and struggles, and strangles her accidentally.

Sadistic murders are sometimes enacted in a dreamlike state. Frederick nearly killed a woman he met at a dance. For many years he had masturbated to a fantasy of tying up a woman after stripping her naked and then assaulting her with a poker. The woman invited him home and in her bedroom 'everything went black'. Only the intervention of a neighbour stopped him from putting his fantasy into practice with fatal results.

Sexual offences against children always arouse public revulsion. Yet child prostitutes of both sexes are still easy to find in Britain and the USA. Many of the so-called victims are willing or semi-willing co-operators, who have already had sexual encounters with adults. Quite often the adult is a relative or friend of the family, which obviously increases any psychological problems the child may have to face later.

Incest is not unusual in our society. Most often a father has intercourse with one or more of his daughters, occasionally his son. Much less frequently a mother's sexual association with her son comes to the notice of the public. There is more chance of its being overlooked than a father/daughter relationship, for it is difficult to prove and, in the majority of cases, stops short of intercourse.

The amount of attention devoted by newspapers to cases of incest, and the intensity of feelings aroused in their readers, suggests that incest, or rather fantasies of incest, play an important role in the formation of sexual fantasies. Men convicted of incest are sometimes given harsh prison sentences. This has no deterrent effect either on the convicted man or on others like him. Can it be regarded in any way but punitive to sentence (in 1973) to five years' imprisonment a man found guilty of incest with his twenty-year-old daughter? Many bank robbers get less. What made this wretched man seem so dangerous to his countrymen? Surely their own sexual fantasies.

Fantasies involving schoolgirls are fairly common among men. A sailor enjoys thinking of fourteen-year-old schoolgirls, dressed in school uniform with round hats and pigtails. In his fantasy he scolds the girls for not being sufficiently tidy and makes one of them unplait her hair. The climax of his pleasure comes when he combs the hair and shows the girl how to plait a tidy pigtail. However, he evinces only 'moderate interest' in real schoolgirls.

Another man is attracted to girls of about ten and spends his lunchtime offering sweets to any he encounters. His fantasy is of feeding chocolates to greedy, plump schoolgirls, and his excitement comes from imagining the feel of their lips on his fingers as they take the sweets into their mouths.

Some men are drawn compulsively to a particular child-woman: Ruskin openly to Rose la Touche, Lewis Carroll in a more disguised way. Nabokov described the feelings and behaviour of such a man's passion for a young girl in his novel *Lolita*. Lolita represents a sexual object that is both forbidden and shocking, which explains why the book provoked such an outcry when it was published. Humbert, the central character in the novel, masturbates by rubbing himself against Lolita or sitting on park benches and peering up the skirts of little girls. Many small boys do this until they realize that it is socially unacceptable.

Do all these unfortunate people fail to achieve reasonable gratification of their needs through masturbation? Does sexual tension build up in them to such a level that the barriers separating fantasy from reality are breached? Perhaps the most important step on the road to criminal perversion is the first time that this happens. The first occasion often arises almost by chance, and only part of the fantasy may be played out. Yet this is enough to generate such excitement and satisfaction as to make repetition highly likely. The first taste of forbidden sex (like the Goblin men's fruit) is all too often followed by a compulsive craving. Next time or the time after that more of the fantasy is played out, until eventually nothing separates fantasy from reality. The pervert and society are now at the mercy of his fantasies.

John Cowper Powys described how, as a boy, he was driving along with his father when he caught sight of an old woman holding a young woman, or so it seemed to him, by the throat. The young woman's head was leaning back in a position that seemed extremely unnatural, 'and the blood rushed to my head'. The vision was immediately incorporated in his masturbation fantasies and transferred itself 'to that invisible "Book of Perdition"'. Yet Powys never allowed his sadistic fantasies to cross the boundaries of reality. Perhaps he was saved in this respect through his writings.

Treatment

If one regards anti-social forms of perversion as illnesses, then it follows that these people need and should have treatment. It is only comparatively recently that criminal sexual behaviour has been looked upon as mental illness, rather than wickedness. Enthusiastic psychiatrists now examine and declare criminals seriously disturbed and in need of prolonged therapy. But as Szasz has noted, everyone is seen to be mentally ill by the overzealous psychiatrist, just as the zealous theologian a century or more ago saw everyone as sinful. But unfortunately the results of treatment are unpredictable and unimpressive. As with alcoholics and drug addicts, the outcome of the treatment depends very much on the strength of the patient's motivation to be cured. And no one abandons willingly and readily something that he feels is needed and that gives so much pleasure. The compulsion to repeat a perversion is probably never wholly lost. It is arguable therefore that people convicted of a serious sadistic sex crime should never be released into the community – at least until more reliable cures are available.

Psychoanalytic treatment is neither a practical nor a particularly effective therapy. Drugs can reduce or take away male sex drive and so can surgery, either on the genitals themselves or on the area of the brain holding the sex centres; but all these are crude and ethically dubious techniques. Claims are made for behaviour therapy, which is based on the view that since sexual perversions are learned they can be unlearned and a more acceptable way of behaviour can be substituted. But the successful treatment of the young psychopath in *A Clockwork Orange* gave a simplified picture of what such treatment might achieve. Alas! at the present time it is not possible to change a deep-seated pattern of behaviour by such means. Not only the object of the pervert's sex drive but the organization of his fantasies, the way he handles his aggressive feelings, his basic psychological needs and disposition, must all be changed in some way. Not until we understand more about our fantasies and their formation can we hope to progress in this matter.

Psychological Effects of Masturbation

Masturbation in childhood without doubt influences the formation of fantasies and later sexual behaviour. But there is no convincing evidence to back up Freud's early belief that it causes fixation and arrests psychic development. The importance of masturbation for a child's development may depend to some extent on his emotional security, particularly on his relationship with the person closest to him, usually his mother. A secure, contented child won't need to fall back continually on his fantasies and masturbate compulsively, as some anxious, unhappy children do. He is less likely to feel strongly and persistently sadistic or masochistic when upset or frustrated. It is the unhappy, insecure child who is most likely to reach adult life with fantasies of a disturbing nature, and consequently run the risk of suffering from sexual disorders.

It is futile to attempt to stop a child from masturbating in the hope of preventing the development of sado-masochistic fantasies. It is equally ridiculous to look upon all childhood masturbation as necessarily a desirable activity. Compulsive masturbation in particular is a warning sign that all is not well with a child's emotional and fantasy life.

Masturbation during adolescence not only helps to relieve tension but gives people time to become accustomed to their fantasies, to compare them with the feelings and experiences of falling in love and passing infatuations. All this is reassuring. But masturbation is not always helpful to the timid adolescent with strictly homosexual fantasies or fantasies of a bizarre and frighteningly anti-social nature. He or she will feel too threatened by such fantasies to masturbate with easy enjoyment, or to relate them in any way to friends and acquaintances.

A sixteen-year-old boy was able to tolerate his fantasy of crucifying, mutilating and raping a woman only by imagining a female friend of his grandmother's in her early seventies. Not until he was in his late twenties was he able to sleep with a middle-aged woman. Eventually he married a woman twenty years older. Through the 'protection' of an older woman, or 'mother figure', he was able to overcome his anxiety and come to terms with his fantasy.

But not everyone fares as well. Some people withdraw increasingly from society into themselves, and come to depend on compulsive masturbation for relief. Their fantasies remain fixed and undeveloped, and they grow ever more narrow and introspective. As time passes it becomes difficult, if not impossible, for them to break out of such a vicious circle.

Others are lucky enough to find themselves a partner, but they have to keep their fantasies in well-separated, watertight compartments. They need to idealize their partner as a protection, and to place him or her on a high pedestal. Inevitably they tend to lack sexual enthusiasm and enjoyment, and some are troubled by impotence or frigidity. Masturbation may become a compulsive need for such people, far surpassing intercourse in desire, pleasure and strength of orgasm. Their fantasies can rarely be disclosed, let alone acted out in any way with a sexual partner. Emotional relationships are never deep, although they are often long-lasting, protected by idealization.

A good-looking young professional man felt compelled for a long time to masturbate at every possibly opportunity. The youngest of a large family, he lived with his mother. He had a reputation as a 'lady killer', although in fact he had never had intercourse with any of his many women friends. He masturbated about once a week with sadistic fantasies of 'inferior' women and prostitutes.

Difficulties arose only when his mother suggested he should marry the daughter of a man she had once loved – 'for my sake, it will make me so happy'. After much procrastination he agreed. At once he began to masturbate compulsively with sadistic homosexual fantasies. In his fantasies he overcame and buggered beautiful young men. Although attracted to his fiancée, he was literally terrified of the idea of intercourse with her, visualizing failure and humiliation. He masturbated in order to blot out heterosexual fantasies and the fear of impotence. But in fact his compulsive masturbation served only to reinforce his anxieties and impotence and cut him off increasingly from his fiancée. Eventually she broke off the engagement.

Jane is a twenty-eight-year-old medical doctor. She derives enormous sensual satisfaction from palpating the bellies of her patients. Her pleasure in this activity goes back to at least the age of seven, soon after her mother explained to her in some detail how children are conceived and born. She undressed her younger brother and prodded his belly so forcefully that he screamed from fright and pain. This developed into a mutually satisfying nightly game. Abdominal palpation was followed by genital massage and the imaginary collection of 'food for babies'. Jane is now a gynaecologist, partly because of worries over the pleasure she obtained from feeling male abdomens. As an extra precaution, among other reasons, she married. After one year of marriage, oral sex, preceded by palpation of her husband's belly, is still her main source of gratification.

It is now generally accepted that masturbation does not itself cause neurosis, but that it may be a neurotic symptom. However the view that all adults who prefer masturbation to intercourse must be neurotic is far too sweeping. Many people fall back on masturbation when emotionally upset or deprived. At least forty per cent of men in Britain and the USA masturbate at some time after their marriage, particularly when their wives are pregnant. Masturbation not only relieves sexual tension but may inadvertently lead them to a better understanding of their underlying problems.

Noel and Lillian, a couple in their forties, had been married for fourteen years. Noel felt increasingly alienated from his wife and critical of her. He resented that she no longer seemed to support him properly at social functions, never tried to make herself look attractive and rarely responded to hints that he wanted to experiment in bed. He threatened to leave her or to take a mistress. In fact he never progressed beyond surreptitiously kissing other women. Then he discovered that Lillian had been having an affair with a neighbour for over three years. His anger and humiliation were intense. He began to masturbate, after many years of abstinence, with fantasies of being assaulted by pretty youths and forced to ejaculate. After orgasm he invariably felt depressed, and during these times he thought about the nature of his fantasy. Gradually he came to see, 'like a cartoon unfolding', how he had humiliated and rejected Lillian throughout their marriage and why she had sought reassurance and comfort in an affair. In consequence his feelings and attitude towards his wife changed and their marital relationship improved.

But not all masturbation is so constructive in its effects. Edmund, a thirty-two-year-old man, was discontented with his marriage. His wife, Sandra, who was still in love with him after six years, tried to please him in every way, waited on him hand and foot at home and leaned over backwards to entertain his business acquaintances and friends. Edmund had had several messy affairs, which he had proudly revealed to Sandra. Every morning after Sandra got up and went downstairs he masturbated to a fantasy of himself humiliating and beating several women. When his wife called out that breakfast was ready he shouted 'coming' and ejaculated. The fantasy he had while masturbating gave him no new insight and served only to reinforce his resentful dependence on his wife.

Apart from such cases, most people probably come to terms with their sexual fantasies by early adulthood and learn to accept them or channel them into activities like work and bringing up a family. Sometimes when these outlets are removed or lose their significance, as when men and women retire, or children grow up and leave home, a period of compulsive masturbation follows. Masturbation at such a time symbolizes a person's depression and despair, his sense of defeat and ultimately his death. Such compulsive masturbation causes people to withdraw ever further into themselves, away from human contact and warmth and feelings. Despair and masturbation encourage one another, and occasionally the vicious circle ends in suicide.

Ever since Mark had been made redundant at work he shut himself away, refusing to see his friends or to go out with his wife. He masturbated several times a day, imagining himself being assaulted in various ways by men and women. He bought pornographic magazines and left them lying about the house. Three months later he left home and drowned himself.

Sometimes the middle-aged compulsive masturbator becomes preoccupied with sex, grows his hair (however thin) long, wears trendy clothes more suitable to his son or daughter and almost overnight changes the habits of a lifetime.

Patrick is in his mid-fifties. Three years ago he had a

heart attack. After recovering he became, to the distress of his wife and children, 'a different man'. He let his hair grow shoulder length, bought a toupé, took to wearing flashy rings and bracelets and occasionally used cheap perfumes. He went to nightclubs, insisted on bringing strange young women home – until his wife threatened divorce – and filled the house with pornographic books and pictures. He talked continuously about sex, about how attractive he was and about his success in picking up 'bunnies'. He walked about his home in the nude and frequently masturbated with every sign of enjoyment in front of his wife. When she told him he was too old to behave in this way he answered: 'We're as young as we feel.'

Patrick is using sex to blot out his anxiety about the future, his fear of further heart attacks, invalidism and death. His fantasies act as a kind of smokescreen, creating an illusion of youth and virility, even as they relentlessly erode his psychological and social foundations. As long as they dominate his thoughts and behaviour he is a doomed man. Perhaps if he had not been so inhibited earlier and had come to terms with his sadistic fantasies before his heart attack he would not have reacted in this way. Perhaps if his wife had accepted her own fantasies early on in the marriage she might now have been able to help her husband and understand his behaviour.

In this case we can see both sides of the problem posed by sex fantasies. Bottled up and suppressed by both Patrick and his wife they resulted in a dull marriage lacking in spontaneity. When Patrick's anxiety about his health was displaced on to sex, pressure from his fantasies became too great and he was no longer able to control them; they took control of him. The lesson to be learned here is that extremes of suppression or open expression are frequently liable to have bad effects, both on the individual and on society.

9 Epilogue—The Fantasy Game

Where is it now, the glory and the dream?
Wordsworth

Sexual fantasies, apart from additional embellishments, have probably altered little over the past thousand years or so. And unless the upbringing of children and the family structure of our society become radically different, it is difficult to imagine much change occurring over the next thousand years.

Those who control or influence other people are in a position to realize their sexual fantasies. For when men and women have power over others they inevitably have the possibility of gratifying their fantasies, directly or indirectly. Fantasies that never reach the light of day can be satisfied only through solitary masturbation. But in the 'real' world they may be gratified directly through emotional relationships, or indirectly by behaviour that appears at first sight to be asexual, but which in fact is really closely linked to sexual fantasy. Sadistic and masochistic fantasies influence our lives in many ways and often determine how we behave to one another. The ability of such fantasies to colour our thoughts and actions subconsciously is not widely enough appreciated, although it is understood all too well by advertisers, propagandists and others who want to take advantage of our gullibility.

Advertising

Today more than ever before an army of experts is busy cashing in on our most primitive inclinations. On all sides our sexual fantasies are stimulated: by films, posters, television advertisements and shows, the theatre, books, modern art, strip cartoons and shop-window displays. Fantasies are cleverly used by advertisers to increase sales of a divergent range of goods, from cars to dog foods.

Oral fantasies, which evoke a particularly high response in men, are ubiquitous – cigarettes, cigars, cosmetics, chocolate bars, clothes and even cough syrup are drawn into them. The association of the product with sexual fantasies invests it with strong emotional feeling and makes it more noticeable to susceptible buyers. In one advertisement for cigars, headed 'Sheer enjoyment', a seductive, scantily clad girl sits in the sea, her mouth invitingly half open, holding a bunch of grapes over one shoulder. Long necklaces of shells dangle from her neck to her navel and give a sado-masochistic flavour to the oral fantasy. In another a 'dirty old man' and a schoolboy perched on his knee push a spoonful of cough syrup into one another's open mouths. Thus that brand of medicine comes to have the appeal of a mutual fellatio scene. Sadistic fantasies are conjured up by the use of black leather and boots, peaked caps, knives and other suggestive objects. Voyeur scenes are particularly popular since they are unlikely to arouse anxiety – the last thing an advertiser wants – as more direct fantasies may do. A typical voyeuristic fantasy concerns a television advertisement for a breakfast cereal. Here the family routine of getting up is evoked by the sixteen-year-old daughter of the household being disturbed in her shower by her younger brother. This brief suggestion of incest cuts to a quick flash of the girl pulling a sweater over her bra before coming down to join the secure and happy family at the breakfast table. Such advertisements fulfil a variety of fantasy needs and stimulate sales of the product associated with them.

There are male and female models to suit all requirements, depending on what the advertiser wants. Many of the Sunday newspaper pictures of women modelling clothes are still aimed at male fantasies. Male masochism is clearly the target, for female models look rapacious and aggressive. In theory at least the stimulated man should buy, or urge his wife/mistress to buy, the goods displayed by the sadistic model.

But increasingly clothes advertisements are geared to titillating women, stimulating their fantasies through identification with the model, allaying the fears of those who see themselves as sexually rapacious, provoking envy, even jealousy, of the model's sexual characteristics and power. And there are now many more provocatively sexy male models – in bulging underpants – to excite the sexually emancipated woman.

What effect does this steady arousal of our sexual fantasies have on the majority of us? Probably the sheer quantity makes it cancel itself out. It may, however, decrease some people's threshold of aggression, and perhaps create a climate in which violence is more readily unleashed, for power and aggression are inseparable from fantasies. Mass fantasies are readily released by disruptive mob behaviour, particularly in peaceful times when there is no outside scapegoat. Many of the outbreaks of violence and vandalism that occur today stem from the release of mass sexual fantasies and their associated aggression. And we all know how prominent people who have the misfortune to be involved in a sexual scandal rapidly become the scapegoats for millions of people's fantasies, and are persecuted mercilessly by the news media.

Sexual fantasies are readily gratified through the idealization of some cause or person. Religion, patriotism, the

Empire, those great ideals that used to harness people's fantasies and channel them in one direction are now dim relics of the past to many people. The IRA and Arab guerrillas still have plenty of scope for satisfying their sexual fantasies. Their ideals and aims create a sado-masochistic paradise. But it is difficult for onlookers, whose fantasies are uninvolved, to recognize that the running battles are part of the fantasy game, that much of the terror tactics, the murder and torture stem from the participants' fantasies rather than from purposeful attempts to gain the upper hand and victory. (One suspects that advertisements using sex fantasies in Northern Ireland are much less influential than in the United Kingdom, because there are such opportunities there for indirect fantasy satisfaction.)

Masturbation

Masturbation is the obvious and simplest way of gratifying fantasies. To a certain (and limited) extent, the masturbator is sexually self-sufficient. And ultimately, in a society such as ours, which worships the sacred cow of communication and family life, this must arouse suspicion and resentment, however harmless the solitary masturbator is to himself and to others. But we would do well to reconsider for a moment the virtues and advantages of masturbation discussed in Chapter 7, and remember that it is not merely a poor substitute for sexual intercourse, but an activity that may sometimes be advantageous to society. The masturbator who really accepts his or her sadistic or masochistic fantasies cannot possibly be smug and censorious about other people's sexual habits, but must feel and express humility and compassion. Undoubtedly, too, many distressing emotional entanglements might be avoided if men and women went in for masturbation before making love to people they knew at heart they were using simply as sexual conveniences or props.

Masturbation usually relieves the physical urge for sex. The accompanying use of sexual fantasies acts, just as non-sexual fantasies do, as a safety valve for those emotional needs that we so often have to repress in the course of our everyday lives. Those people who are not reconciled to this side of their nature may feel self-disgust and depression after masturbation, but some also feel this after experiencing orgasms with their lover. A sense of loneliness momentarily makes itself felt to them. Proust – a lonely, unhappy man, at odds with his sadistic fantasies – was undoubtedly describing this feeling when he wrote: 'The bonds that unite another person to ourselves exist only in our mind . . . and notwithstanding the illusion by which we would fain be cheated and with which, out of love . . . we cheat other people, we exist alone. Man is the creature that cannot emerge from himself, that knows his fellows only in himself . . .'

A loving sexual relationship is of course the most satisfying and satisfactory way, but inevitably only a momentary one, of fusing fantasy and reality, and of allowing the associated emotions of fantasy, of sadism or masochism, to be gratified. Indeed, as we saw in Chapter 4, love and lust feed on one another and work together to enhance and strengthen a good marital or other sexual relationship.

Indirect Gratification

Frequently suppressed sexual fantasies seek to achieve outlets and satisfaction in indirect ways. People with masochistic fantasies strive for power and admiration; sadists struggle for positions of authority within the safety of a powerful organization.

The masochist's overwhelming need for power is frequently disguised by his idealism. Marx, Lenin, Napoleon, Hitler, Churchill, Mussolini, Gandhi, de Gaulle – the list of masochists is endless. So long as the masochist continues to struggle for his ideal all is well. Indeed without the masochist the world would be a different, if not a lesser place. Success in gaining his goal at once alters the equilibrium between reality and fantasy. With victory attained, the masochistic leader gradually loses sight of his original aims. W. H. Auden put it well:

Standing among the ruins, the horror-struck conqueror
    exclaimed:
Why do they have to attempt to refuse me my destiny? Why?

The successful masochist's fantasies come increasingly and unwittingly to dominate his behaviour and distort his original aims. He needs to feel secure and all-powerful and he will brook no rivals. He calls on himself and the people he has chosen to lead – who may well have chosen him as their leader as much because of the influence of their mass fantasies as for realistic reasons – for ever greater sacrifices and dedication. He and they must love one another to the death. Since he is a hero, his people must also have heroic powers of endurance.

His lieutenants and the bureaucrats he establishes in power are only too happy to interpret and carry out his wishes, protected by his authority. All too often these minor officials have sadistic fantasies, which they can now gratify in the name of their leader. Hardship, suffering, the secret police, torture, inequality grow, and idealism becomes a mere loathsome word.

All revolutions and wars must fail in their original aims because of the distorting effect of the victors' fantasies. The French and Russian revolutions, the Nazi and fascist regimes, the Spanish civil war – in every case the original idealistic aims were quickly lost sight of, the new regime's activities became increasingly coloured by the fantasies of its leaders. Economic and social factors are of course concerned in any revolution or dramatic social change, but it is impossible to be idealistic or optimistic about the outcome of social upheavals when it is so clear that men's sexual fantasies will expect their due reward once peace has been restored to the scene. Wagner symbolized this human problem in *The Ring*. Men, like the gods of Valhalla, find themselves unable to pay the giants they have employed to build their castles in the air. Until we learn to control them and employ them sensibly, we are liable to meet our *Götterdämmerung* time after time.

The young Beatrice Webb was an idealist. She wrote: 'I have staked all on the emotional goodness of human nature.' Many years later, disillusioned, she commented: 'I realize how permanent are the evil impulses and instincts in man – how little you can count on changing some of these – for instance the greed of wealth and power . . .'

But it is naïve and unconstructive to look on human nature as being essentially good or bad. Man's sexual fantasies can be put to good or bad use, or even not used at all in relation to his fellows. It is a cliché that all power corrupts. The corollary of this is that men are 'decent' and good only when they are powerless. For once men or women have power, they are immediately in a position to gratify their fantasies, however indirectly. There are few people capable of standing back and observing their behaviour with detachment, or recognizing their disguised fantasies, and doing something about it. No one could wish to remove or suppress our fantasies totally because much good stems from them. It is the socially harmful effects that need to be understood and controlled.

A truly egalitarian society is possible only when the members of that society can no longer be used as objects for the gratification of their fellow men's sexual fantasies. If sexual permissiveness means that we are achieving a better understanding of our fantasies, then long live permissiveness. But there is nothing to suggest that this is so. Rather it seems possible that some aspects of sexual permissiveness, by stimulating fantasies, encourage violence and the use of indirect methods of gratification.

Sooner or later, if we are to survive as reasonably free people and not become subjected to totalitarian systems, men and women must learn to accept their fantasies, to become aware of their powers and therefore able to use them constructively. The first step must be to come to terms with our fantasies. Today's teenagers and young adults admit to masturbation without the sense of guilt and shame recorded by such people as Julian Huxley, Graham Greene and Bertrand Russell during their adolescence. But shutters come down rapidly enough when you inquire about their fantasies.

Perhaps in some future 1984 world everyone will be tested in childhood and typed for fantasy, just as people are today for intelligence or blood groups. The strength of everyone's masochistic or sadistic fantasy, no doubt measured like an IQ test, would be known to all. At that point we would have reached the second millennium. And the fantasy game will be over.

References

Page   Line

40   26   Sigmund Freud, *Three Essays on the Theory of Sexu-*
             ality (Hogarth Press, 1962)
42   1   Joachim C. Fest, *Hitler* (Weidenfeld & Nicolson, 1974)
47   24   Cecil Woodham-Smith, *Florence Nightingale* (Penguin,
             1955)
53   32   'The way we fight now', *Times Literary Supplement*
             (1 March 1974)
65   19   *The Diary of Samuel Pepys*, vol. iv, ed. Robert Latham
             & William Matthews (Bell, 1971)

             CHAPTER 3
             General reading:
             Milton Diamond, 'A Critical Evaluation of the On-
             togeny of Human Sexual Behaviour', *The Quarterly*
             Review of Biology, 40 (1965), 147–75
             Gender Differences: their ontogeny and significance,
             ed. C. Ounsted & D. C. Taylor (Churchill Livingstone,
             1972)
             Corinne Hutt, *Males and Females* (Penguin, 1972)
             J. Money, J. G. Hampson, J. C. Hampson, 'Hermaphro-
             ditism', *Bulletin of John Hopkins Hospital*, 97 (1955),
             284–300.
             Alfred C. Kinsey *et al.*, *Sexual Behaviour in the Human*
             Male (W. B. Saunders, Philadelphia & London, 1948)
             Alfred C. Kinsey *et al.*, *Sexual Behaviour in the Human*
             Female (W. B. Saunders, Philadelphia & London,
             1953)
             Sex and Behaviour, ed. Frank A. Beach (John Wiley,
             1965)
             An Analysis of Human Sexual Response, ed Ruth &
             Edward Brecher (Panther, 1968)
             Masters, W. H. & Johnson, V. E., *Human Sexual*
             Response (Churchill, 1966)
71   30   Sigmund Freud, *Three Essays on the Theory of*
             Sexuality (Hogarth Press, 1962)

             CHAPTER 4
82   15   *The Song of Songs*, 4:1
83   22   Philip Sydney, 'The Bargain', no. 45 in *New Oxford*

Page Line

Book of English Verse 1250–1950, ed. Helen Gardner
(Clarendon Press, 1972)

83   28   Alfred Tennyson, 'Mariana', *Poems and Plays* (O.U.P.,
1971) p. 7

CHAPTER 5
General reading:
Steven Marcus, *The Other Victorians* (Corgi, 1970)
*The Report of the Commission on Obscenity and Por-
nography* (Bantam, 1970)
Alan Burns, *To Deprave and Corrupt* (Davis-Poynter,
1972)
E. Kronhausen & P. Kronhausen, *Pornography and
the Law* (Ballantine, New York, 1959)
Rachel Anderson, *The Purple Heart Throbs* (Hodder,
1974)
Lord Longford, *Introduction to Pornography*, *The
Longford Report* (Coronet, 1972)

102   9   Anonymous verse, *Faber Book of Children's Verse*,
compiled by Janet Adam Smith (Faber, 1963)

113   24ff *Christina Rossetti's Verse*, selected and introduced by
Elizabeth Jennings (Faber, 1970)

115   1   Sigmund Freud, *Three Essays on the Theory of
Sexuality* (Hogarth Press, 1962)

115   16   Edward Lucie-Smith, *Eroticism in Western Art*
(Thames & Hudson, 1972)

116   4   Lord Longford, *op. cit.*

116   8   *The Case against Pornography*, ed. David Holbrook
(Tom Stacey, 1972)

116   10   Alex Comfort, *The Anxiety Makers* (Panther,
1968)

117   13   David Holbrook in *The Times* (26 August 1971)

117   18   L. Rosen & S. H. Turner, *J. Sex Research* 5.235
(1969)

117   27   H. J. Eysenck, *Psychology is about People* (Allen Lane,
1972)

119   12   Lord Longford, 'Pornography, What's to be done?',
The Sunday Times (7 November 1971)

121   11   Edward Lucie-Smith, *op. cit.*

Page Line

CHAPTER 6

General reading:

H. R. Trevor-Roper, *Religion, The Reformation and Social Change*, chapter 3 'The European Witch Craze of the 16th and 17th Centuries' (Macmillan, 1967)

Richard Barber, *The Knight and Chivalry* (Longman, 1970)

Gregory Zilboorg, *A History of Medical Psychology* (W. W. Norton, 1941)

Witchcraft, Confessions and Accusations, ed. Mary Douglas particularly chapters 1, 2, 3 & 4 (Tavistock Publications, 1970)

Katherine M. Rogers, *The Troublesome Helpmate. A History of Misogyny in Literature* (Washington University Press, 1966)

125	6	William Dunbar, quoted from *The Troublesome Helpmate*.
125	25	Quoted from '*Not in God's Image*', ed. Julia O'Faolain & Lauro Martines (Temple Smith, 1973)
125	31	Roger de Caen, quoted from *The Troublesome Helpmate*.
126	6	Richard Rolle, quoted from *The Troublesome Helpmate*.
128	19	H. R. Trevor-Roper, *op. cit.*
128	29ff	*Malleus Malificarum*, quoted from Zilboorg, *op. cit.*
129	6ff	Quoted from Zilboorg, *op. cit.*
131	23	Quoted from Zilboorg, *op. cit.*
132	18	Alan Macfarlane, from *Witchcraft, Confessions and Accusations*.
132	29	Paul Boyer, Stephen Nissenbaum, *Salem Possessed. The Social Origins of Witchcraft* (Harvard University Press, 1974)

CHAPTER 7

General reading:

E. H. Hare, 'Masturbatory Insanity: The History of an Idea' *Journal of Mental Science* 108 (January 1962)

Thomas S. Szasz, *The Manufacture of Madness* (Routledge & Kegan Paul, 1971)

Page Line

Geoffrey Best, *Mid-Victorian Britain* (Weidenfeld & Nicolson, 1971)

Duncan Crow, *The Victorian Woman* (Allen & Unwin, 1971)

Constance Rover, *Love, Morals and the Feminists* (Routledge & Kegan Paul, 1970)

W. E. Houghton, *The Victorian Frame of Mind* (Yale University Press, 1957)

G. M. Young, *Victorian England, Portrait of an Age* (O.U.P., 1957)

David M. Feldman, *Birth Control in Jewish Law* (New York University Press, 1968)

Kellow Chesney, *The Victorian Underworld* (Temple Smith, 1970)

Richard Hunter & Ida MacAlpine, *Three Hundred Years of Psychiatry* 1535–1860 (O.U.P., 1963)

148 31 Quoted from Feldman, *op. cit.*

149 1 *Ibid.*

149 26 Richard Baxter, quoted from Hunter & MacAlpine, *op. cit.*

152 15 F. A. Voltaire, *Oeuvres Complétes*, vol. 42, *Dictionnaire Philosophique*, 'Onan, Onanisme' (Paris, 1784)

152 24 John Hunter, quoted from Hunter & MacAlpine, *op. cit.*

153 16 Benjamin Rush, *Medical Inquiries and Observations upon the Diseases of the Mind* (Hafner, New York, 1962)

153 27 P. Pinel, *A Treatise on Insanity* (Hafner, New York, 1962)

153 30 E. Esquirol, quoted from Hare, *op. cit.*

154 6 Quoted from Hare, *op. cit.*

154 16 Samuel Howe, quoted from Hunter & MacAlpine, *op. cit.*

155 24 Havelock Ellis, *Psychology of Sex* (Heinemann, 1933)

156 23 Sandor Ferenczi, *Further Contributions to the Theory and Technique of Psychoanalysis* (Institute of Psycho-analysis & Hogarth Press, 1926)

157 1 Sigmund Freud, *Three Essays on the Theory of Sexuality*.

Page   Line

157   25   'The Discussion of 1912 on Masturbation and our
             Present Day Views', *Psychoanalytic Study of the
             Child*, vol. vi, ed. Anna Freud *et al.* (Hogarth Press,
             1951)
158   19   Charles Rycroft, *Wilhelm Reich*, (Fontana, 1972)
158   33   Wilhelm Stekel, *Autoeroticism* (Peter Nevill, New
             York, 1951)

CHAPTER 8
General reading:
Michael Balint, *Problems of Human Pleasure and
Behaviour* (Hogarth Press, 1957)
Havelock Ellis, *The Psychology of Sex* (Heinemann,
1933)
G. Gorer, *Sex and Marriage in England Today*
(Nelson, 1971)
Helene Deutsch, *The Psychology of Women* (Grune &
Stratton, New York, 1945)

Quiz

At my publisher's request I offer this short quiz. It should be taken not as a serious scientific test but rather as a lighthearted guide with which the reader can examine his or her own fantasies and inhibitions. All questions should be answered quickly.

PART ONE: SADOMASOCHISTIC SCORE

1 How do you think your friends and colleagues estimate the quality of your work?
a Overestimate it
b Underestimate it
c Neither

2 Could you see yourself dying for an ideal or cause in which you passionately believe?
a Yes
b No

3 With a close friend would you rather
a Give a present
b Receive one

4 However well you drive, when you are overtaken on the open road, are you
a Irritated or angry
b Don't mind in the least

5 Would you rather be
a Famous and miserable
b Unsuccessful but content

6 Given a strict choice between saving the life of a good friend and one hundred strangers, will you
a Save your friend
b Save the strangers

7 Your lover, spouse or child is drowning and you cannot swim. Will you
a Jump in and try and save him or her
b Run to a nearby telephone and dial for help

8 In a murder trial would you rather be
a A famous lawyer, persuading the jury by your argument
b The judge summing up the facts and passing sentence
c One of the jury

9 Would you rather be
  a The planner of a great bank robbery

  b The senior detective trying to bring the robbers to justice

10 Are you irritated by having to conform to customs and conventions?
   a Yes
   b No

11 Do you want want to outdo your father or mother?
   a Yes
   b No

12 Do you agree with Abraham Lincoln that the ballot is stronger than the bullet?
   a Yes
   b No

13 *For Women.* Are you attracted to a man who, like Lord Byron, is mad, bad and dangerous to know?
   a Yes
   b No

   For Men. Are you attracted to the regal woman who longs to be dominated by her male partner?
   a Yes
   b No

14 Do you find the idea that you might kill or seriously harm someone
   a Absurd
   b Terrifying
   c Neither

15 Life is just a wild goose chase. Do you agree?
   a Yes
   b No

16 Were you terribly let down as a child?
   a Yes
   b No

17 Do you enjoy playing a game or sport as much if you lose as if you win?
   a Yes
   b No

18 Do you think that everyone has to fight for his own position in life?
   a Yes
   b No

19 You see your six-year-old-son or nephew pulling the wings off captive flies. Do you
   a Immediately punish him
   b Reason with him
   c Feel unconcerned about such a commonplace happening

PART TWO: INHIBITION SCORE

1 Are you or were you ashamed of masturbating?
  a Yes
  b No
  c You never did it

2 Do you think your sexual fantasies are abnormal?
  a Yes
  b No
  c You never had any

3 Do you
a Discuss your sexual fantasies openly with your,
partner
b Hint at them indirectly
c Never mention them

4 Would you be ashamed of
being seen either buying or
reading pornography?
a Yes
b No

5 Do you read newspaper accounts of sexual irregularities
and offences
a With open enjoyment
b With some discomfort
c Don't read them

6 Are you ashamed of being seen
urinating by
a A spouse
b A close friend
c Anyone
d No

7 Would you like to experiment
with new sexual techniques
with your partner?
a Yes
b No

8 Would you be shocked if your
partner suggested a third
person, of either sex, should
join you in bed?
a Yes
b No
c Just cross

ANSWERS

PART ONE

1 a S2
   b M2
   c S1
2 a M3
   b S1
3 a M1
   b S2
4 a M3
   b S2
5 a M3
   b S2
6 a M2
   b S2
7 a M3
   b S1

8 a M3
   b S2
   c S1
9 a M2
   b S2
10 a M1
   b S2
11 a M2
   b o
12 a o
   b M3
13 a M3
   b S2
14 a S1
   b M2
   c o
15 a S1
   b M1

16 a S2
   b o
17 a S1
   b M3
18 a M2
   b S1
19 a S2
   b M1
   c S1

PART TWO

1 a 2
   b o
   c 1
2 a 2
   b o
   c 1

3 a o
   b 1
   c 2
4 a 2
   b o
5 a o
   b 1
   c 2
6 a 3
   b 2
   c 1
   d o
7 a 2
   b o
8 a 2
   b o
   c 1

ANALYSIS OF SCORES

The total score possible for masochism is 40. The average masochism score lies between 15 and 25. Above 25, masochistic fantasies are strongly developed and play an important part in influencing your life. A score of 30 and above suggests an idealistic, romantic nature, great ambition and drive to succeed, a tendency to be easily depressed by failure, and a strong need to feel loved.

Men of this type marry emotionally strong women, but they do not make easy husbands. They need to be continually reassured that women like and admire them. Since they find it difficult to reject or distress an admiring woman, it is all too easy for them to drift into affairs. A woman of this type can be as ambitious and ruthless in work as men. She is liable to idealize her sexual partner and attribute God-like qualities to him. She is a one-man woman, able to relate her fantasy needs fully to her husband or lover, possessive and jealous. Yet for this to continue the man must seem to be outwardly strong and successful. She moulds him, in her imagination, to fit her needs. Group sex and couple-swapping are not for those with high masochism scores.

A high inhibition score (9+) which is very likely when either masochism or sadism is strongly marked, increases these characteristics. For instance, a man with a score of M34, S5, inhibition 10, is likely to be very successful in his work but suffer great difficulties in his sexual and emotional life.

Everyone has some degree of sadism, counterbalancing, modifying and modified by masochism. A very low or high score for sadism correlates with a correspondingly high or low masochism score.

The total score for sadism is 28. The average sadism score ranges from 6 to 10. Above 14, sadistic fantasies are strongly developed and, when combined with a high inhibition score, result in an excessive degree of self-control. Emotions, particularly relating to anger, are bottled up, impulsive or risky actions are eschewed, and routine and orderliness encouraged. Both men and women work hard and conscientiously and need to earn praise from their superiors. They do not have the warmth of feeling and spontaneity of the strong masochist, and people do not confide in them or trust them naturally. Often, although respected, they are feared by their colleagues and underlings. Although they may be very capable and achieve promotion, they do not aspire to top leadership; but they make excellent seconds-in-command, functioning well so long as they are sheltered by a superior.

Men expect their wives to conform to a routine; any upset at home is liable to result in abuse and even physical violence. They make unadaptable fathers and their teenage children frequently rebel. Women with high sadism, like men, are excellent workers but unlike their masochistic opposites, they don't allow themselves to become over-involved in their work or with their employers. Affairs or marriage are more often of a cerebral rather than a passionate nature. They tend to choose reliable, non-heroic husbands. They don't, by choice, have large families; compulsive pregnancies require a high degree of masochism. Group and experimental sex, since they can be viewed with detachment, are enjoyable to many people with predominantly sadistic fantasies.

Index

actors, fantasies of, 54–5
adolescence, fantasies during, 70–71, 81
alcoholics, fantasies of, 38
alcoholism, compensating partner's impotence, 63
Alekhine, 62
Alexander the Great, 54
Ali, Mohammed, 61, 62
ambition, masochists and, 35
anaesthetists, fantasies of, 47
anal masturbation, 136
anal rape, in women's fantasies, 10
Anderson, Rachel, 109
Anne, Princess, 65
anonymous letters, 19
anonymous telephone calls, 19, 58
anti-Semitism, 43, 122
anxiety, as cause of masturbation, 137; children's fantasies and, 3
Aristophanes, 146
armed services, fantasies in, xi, 52–4
Arnold, Thomas, 16–17
arson, fantasies and, 21, 52
art, erotic, 114–15
au pair girls, in women's fantasies, 10
Aubrey, John, 137

Barclay, Florence, 108
Barrett Browning, Elizabeth, 69
barristers, and fantasies of, 56–7
baseball, fantasy and, 61
Baxter, Richard, 149–50
Beard, George Miller, 155
beating, *see* flagellation; spanking
Beethoven, Ludwig van, 138
Berlioz, Hector, 138
bestiality, 9, 105
bisexual fantasies, 10
biting, 6, 18
Bleuler, E., 154n.
Bluebeard, 160–61
bomb-hoaxers, fantasies of, 58
Bond, James, 111–13
bondage, masochistic fantasies, 14
Boniface, Saint, 128
Bormann, Martin, 43
boxing, and fantasy, 61
Brady, Ian, 49–50
Braun, Eva, 42
breast-feeding, and masochistic fantasies, 7
bridge players, and fantasy, 61
Brontë, Emily, 84, 103
Broughton, Rhoda, 109
Browning, Penini, 69
Buchanan, John, 44